Integrity of Heart

12 Indestructible Pillars to Build a Successful Life

By Paul F. Davis

Integrity is a topic too rarely talked about in society, schools, the workplace and places of worship. Parents often focus on discipline and achievement, but sometimes fail to mention the importance of patience, perseverance and maintaining integrity en route to success. In other words, what good is it if you exert great effort to climb the ladder of success only to later discover that your ladder is leaning upon the wrong building?

This sadly is the current state of affairs in the United States, among the most populated and influential countries on earth, but financially bankrupt and crumbling within due to poor leadership and corruption in Congress. Our nation cannot even cooperatively work with the President because Congressional officials are susceptible to bribes and manipulation by corporations, as shown by a Stanford University study regarding insider trading on Capitol Hill reported on the TV show *60 Minutes*.

The height of hypocrisy is to impose laws upon the people of a country that the leaders who legislate and draft the laws themselves don't adhere to. Such is the case in the United States where backroom negotiations and deals in Congressional departments occur, seconds after which the very same Congressional officials call their financial planners and stock brokers to maneuver and shift their investments around to monetize the moment and profit on their insider information. Yet were we the American citizens to do the same, we like Martha Stewart would go to jail. The politicians in Washington however are exempt from the same ethical standards.

Thus our national leaders are often despised and disrespected, sometimes even loathed. For years half of the people in the United States have not even participated in elections and exerted any effort to vote. Feeling alienated and unimportant, many are disenchanted with the whole political process, considering it nothing more than lip service and a vain show. Comedian Jay Leno has said, "Politics is show business for ugly people."

More than ugly, many are also greedy. The pretense of public service is evident when the Stanford University study challenged politicians in Washington to sign a bill that would no longer exempt them from insider trading laws.

Only seven Congressional officials signed the bill. In other words Congress likes being able to access such insider information and invest accordingly to profit handsomely. Remove that benefit of "serving" in Congress and many of our present day "leaders" would no longer be desirous of "serving" the American people. Hence the revolving door between politics and business.

Former President George W. Bush installed many business executives (from industries such as oil and gas) into the Environmental Protection Agency leading positions. I'm sure you can guess what happened and was the result? The environment was jeopardized, compromised and not protected. Yet the agency on the surface remained in operation, but the people running it were disinterested in the EPA's founding mission and instead sought to pursue their own corporate objectives driven by a profit motive. Robert Kennedy Jr. wrote about it in *Vanity Fair*, calling it the *Texas Chainsaw Management*.

http://www.vanityfair.com/politics/features/2007/05/revolvingdoor200705

When things precious to life as the environment, our food supply and water security are so easily compromised and disregarded by Congress and corporations, both whom themselves survive from these very elements essential to sustaining life; we have a real problem and lack of values in our land.

When hydraulic fracking for natural gas (shale gas) beneath water aquifers risks the integrity of the water we drink, so much so a documentary film titled *Gasland* showed residents in upstate New York and elsewhere throughout the country where fracking occurred able to light their water on fire within their homes; we have sold ourselves to the extent of cutting short our very lives.

http://tinyurl.com/b6cyy4g

It's no wonder illness and diseases such as cancer, diabetes and heart disease are on the rise across the United States. You don't have to look far to find the source of our public health problems. Farmers have forsaken biodiversity to pursue monoculture hoping to enlarge their profit margins. Much of this was brought about by reason of companies like Monsanto, a pesticide and herbicide manufacturer (and the creator of agent orange used in Vietnam, a country I visited in the summer of 2011, where I witnessed the repercussions of ecocide – three and four generations of children born with deformities still plagued by the deadly chemicals sprayed from airplanes on their land during the Vietnam war decades ago).

Yet today Monsanto has engineered genetically modified seed (with the help of Justice Clarence Thomas a former attorney for Monsanto now "serving" on the U.S. Supreme Court) incorporating it's pesticide within corn, canola, cotton and soy so when farmers spray pesticides and herbicides on their crops; they will be better able to withstand the deadly chemicals, because the seed themselves now have the very same toxic chemicals embedded within them. Such is what many Americans (and the countries we export this foul "food" to abroad) are now eating.

Again it is no surprise we are ill and the current generation is not living as long as their forefathers who preceded them. Skin ailments are understandably on the rise as our bodies are trying to excrete and remove the foul "food" junking up our livers, kidneys and organs. The cost of cheap food is widespread cancer, which one in three in our generation are said to have in one form or another. My book on natural cancer cure and prevention strategies can help if this is something you are suffering with or someone you love.

Such is the result of selling ourselves for a quick buck and short lived profit. We seem to forget our health is priceless. All of our flag waving, phraseology like "God bless America" and political slogans are empty when we merely purport and don't truly mean, nor live by the values we profess (or at least publicly display during election years to curry public favor and get votes for our "cause").

Politicians in bed with the military-industrial-complex tell us to "support the troops" as they run off to invade nations in the Middle East rich with oil and gas. Meanwhile other nations with far more heinous and evil dictators oppressing them in Africa go untouched. Why? Because there are no oil and gas resources to be gained from our invasion, occupation and of course "liberation" in some impoverished parts of Africa.

Back home the shameful reality is we really don't "support the troops" as we say. Camp Lejeune, the Marines largest military base has known for years (some say even a decade or more) that benzene is in the water supply causing both military troops and their families living on the military base cancer and leukemia. Yet nothing has been done to remedy the wrong and protect families from this contaminated water.

http://tinyurl.com/afshycx

Even Coca Cola had benzoic acid in its soda pop until 2008, not realizing (or maybe they did and didn't care until lawsuits awakened them), which combined with ascorbic acid creates benzene – the same petrochemical significantly reduced in allowable quantities in gasoline in the 1970s once it was determined to cause leukemia and cancer.

Yet Coca Cola and Pierre water both had benzoic acid in them (as did I'm sure other carbonated drinks for years). Hence the poor and sad state of our public health across the United States. Meanwhile the media worries about terrorists thousands of miles away, while we eat foul food here at home and are killing ourselves daily.

How ignorant are we as a nation? As we bicker about political ideology and create a culture of fear demonizing and labeling terrorists abroad, at home we are being ravished by polluted water (with fluoride and other heavy metals, the former which much of Europe removed from their water supply decades ago) and foul food. Our mineral depleted soil (lacking in magnesium and selenium thanks to all the spraying of herbicides and pesticides) is unable to produce the quality of agriculture the previous generation knew, so today our immune systems are weakened as we live off processed food.

Processed food is fast and cheap for food companies to make, having a longer shelf life while shortening the lives of consumers. Cigarette companies now have bought food manufacturers, making food the new drug, wherein we now find mind-altering excitotoxins (much of the reason for migraines and mental disorders) to make us food addicts (and thus obese beyond measure).

http://tinyurl.com/bc5t5h4

Preservatives keep the food on the shelf and "safe" but also prevent us from being able to digest, assimilate and readily eliminate that which we eat. The result in turn is a constipated country with foul food rotting within them. Skin disorders and diseases therefore abound.

The *Business of Being Born* is a very revealing documentary exposing how the American medical industry monetizes the moment and preys on mothers when they are most vulnerable and giving birth. Injecting petosin and other drugs into mothers, they soon lose all control, after which doctors can freely perform other costly "interventions" and "help" make themselves and hospitals money.

http://tinyurl.com/ba6gexq

Vaccinations are becoming so widespread and heinous that Robert Kennedy Jr. himself had to admit that when he was a kid, he got between 4 to 6 vaccinations. Alternatively, Kennedy's children received around 22 vaccines. Vaccinations can prove life-altering for some children causing mental disorders, health complications and debilitating diseases. Yet the Center for Disease Control likes to tout vaccines as the cure all to prevent disease, when in reality widespread outbreaks of the flu and various viruses continue unabated even after countless people have received these vaccines.

http://tinyurl.com/b9ubcnj

U.S. soldiers themselves have become violent after taking Larium and Mefloquine, anti-malarial drugs that can cause hallucinations, mood swings, nightmares and brain damage. Yet the CDC is making too much money off all of these drugs to take any responsibility, or recommend the soldiers simply use mosquito nets and trash the drugs. Some soldiers have even killed their wives while taking the anti-malarial drugs.

http://www.cbsnews.com/2100-500164_162-538144.html

http://www.armytimes.com/news/2012/04/military-new-concerns-antimalaria-doxycycline-mefloquine-041112w/

But we are a "free" country we tell ourselves. Oh really? How free is a person overtaken by disease? How free is a country eaten up by cancer? How free is a country overcome by fear that it's very own people fear traveling abroad to enjoy their life? How free is a country when the image we project to the world is one of ignorance and hate? How free is a country when retired military return home and suffer with post-traumatic stress disorder and go into a Sikh temple to kill innocent people thinking them to be Muslims? How free is a country where socially dysfunctional people on mind altering psychiatric drugs (further worsening the problem and intensifying their self-hatred and rage) can so easily buy a gun to use to kill first grade children in a state such as Connecticut?

How "free" is a country that allows pharmaceutical corporations to push their pills on small children to make them dope addicts for life?

These are the hard questions we must ask ourselves. Trying times demand tough decisions, soul searching discussions, and thorough analysis as to what we should do to reform our country.

Integrity of heart is a foundational attitude and disposition I encourage all to cultivate, embrace and adopt in their daily lives. As Jesus Christ said, "Do unto others as you would have them to unto you" (Luke 6:31). This certainly is more easily said than done. Nevertheless if you will sincerely endeavor to make the effort, God will be with and help you every step of the way (and favor and bless your life as you maintain and strive for purity of heart and life).

"Blessed are the pure in heart; they shall see God" (Matthew 5:8). There is no greater blessing than seeing and feeling the Presence of Almighty God with you. "In the Presence of God there is fullness of joy …and pleasures forevermore" (Psalm 16:11).

It is far better to go to sleep with peace at night, than to be looking over your shoulder having to sleep with one eye open (as one drug dealer, a former high school friend, who took a turn for the worst …influenced by his chemist uncle who led him astray sadly; resulting in him being imprisoned for 10 years for selling illegal drugs).

Years ago when working as a lifeguard and driving to a waterpark in Orlando, I saw this former high-school friend on the highway. He had a black eye after having been beaten up. The lesson here is when you walk with shady characters and participate in unwholesome endeavors your life will be less than enjoyable and hard. Truly the Bible warns us: "The way of the transgressor is hard" (Proverbs 13:15).

The dictionary defines integrity as incorruptibility, soundness, completeness and a firm adherence to a code of values. When doing what is right and living with a clean conscience is your goal, you will have a pure heart and less emotional entanglements. Entanglements of the soul and emotional baggage often come about by reason of our own wrongdoing, unethical and poor behavior, which we later regret and feel bad about.

Incorruptibility means you are impenetrable by temptation and incapable of being seduced or swayed to deviate from your purity of heart and moral character. When you have a moral compass prepositioned and a disposition locked in to do that which is right, the appearance of temptation does not appeal to you, neither does it for a split second cause you to question or consider any other alternatives than doing that which is upright.

The blessing of being and living upright is the favor of God, wealth and honor. 'For the LORD God is a sun and shield: the LORD will give grace and glory: no good thing will he withhold from them that walk uprightly' (Psalm 84:11).

God likes to bless and favor those who walk uprightly. This is not to say you have to be perfect, just have a perfect and pure heart desirous of doing that which is right. David was a man after God's heart, but he was imperfect. David committed both adultery and murder, for which God judged him, but David was always quick to repent and embrace the discipline of God for his wrongdoing?

Are you like that? Do you embrace the chastisement of the Lord, as would a child his father's correction? Our heavenly Father loves us and disciplines us for our own good, to prevent us from afflicting ourselves further by reason of our disobedience and stupidity. God knows the beginning from the end, He being the Alpha and Omega. The all wise God, the ancient of days, therefore has our best interest at heart and endeavors to impart wisdom to our hearts to improve and enhance our lives, not remove joy from us, but increase our happiness and give us life more abundantly (see John 10:10).

'Praise the LORD. Blessed is the man that fears the LORD, that delights greatly in His commandments. His seed shall be mighty upon the earth: the generation of the upright shall be blessed. Wealth and riches shall be in his house: and his righteousness endures forever. Unto the upright there arises light in the darkness: he is gracious, and full of compassion, and righteous' (Psalm 112:1-4).

Jesus is the light of the world and when we love, honor, and invite Christ into our hearts and lives; He illuminates our paths, fills us with His purposes, and propels us forward with supernatural power and divine force to live fulfilling and fun lives!

The blessed Holy Spirit is the spirit of wisdom and revelation (Ephesians 1), sent by God to teach us all things (John 14:26) and reveal the fullness of the blessing of Christ to us. Moreover Christ by the power of the Holy Spirit that raised Him from the dead, when dwelling within us, will cause glory and joy to radiate from within (Colossians 1:27) and compel us Godward.

When you have an intimate and tender relationship with the blessed Holy Spirit within your heart, a spirit-to-spirit connection (see Romans 8:16) it is not so easy to live ungodly, unethically and behave inappropriately. The Holy Spirit births holiness in our hearts (see Romans 1:4, Philippians 2:12-13; Zechariah 4:6) constraining and keeping us in the ways of God if we will listen and in humility yield to His wooing, guidance and direction.

Truly 'the fear of the Lord is the instruction of wisdom; and before honor is humility' (Proverbs 15:33). Cultivating humility daily, learning to listen without speaking hastily, harnessing your emotions before responding prematurely, and renewing your mind to think godly is a daily effort. Yet when we decide and predetermine to proactively do so, countless blessings and breakthroughs accompany our obedience and commitment to live in purity and integrity of heart.

When we honor, recognize and acknowledge God in all things (see Proverbs 3:5-6); inquiring of our Creator before making any critical decisions and embarking upon any endeavor, He is faithful and just to lead, guide and speak to us. God can speak to you directly within your heart by His Holy Spirit. God may quietly speak to you through people you know, or strangers on the street with whom you cross paths and interact. It's truly amazing how many random people and circumstances God can use to subtly and gently whisper truth to you and sow spiritual seed in your heart.

God truly knows how to repeatedly speak to us until without a doubt we know it is our Creator and the Lord of life speaking. God knows how to intervene and interrupt situations, interject His thoughts into conversations, and inwardly awaken us and impart direction.

Along with divine direction also comes times of correction. Times of correction should not be shunned, resisted or diminished because they require you to acknowledge change is necessary. Though temporarily uncomfortable, making course corrections in the long run prove to be helpful, less painful and life enhancing. Otherwise if you were to continue traveling and journeying down a dead end path, you will prolong your pain and heartache. Therefore be thankful and grateful when God interrupts your present pattern to prevent you from enduring a life of pain and destruction.

Beyond keeping a tender and humble heart, we must always remember God is in heaven and we on the earth. His thoughts and ways are above ours, they producing more peace, pleasure and prosperity if we will only humbly embrace and trust Almighty God.

'By humility and the fear of the Lord are riches, honor, and life' (Proverbs 22:4). When we get the first things right – that is humility and a healthy respect to reverence God; then the usual things society readily seeks after such as riches, honor and long life take care of themselves and show up for us.

When I was asked to speak in Orange County, California in 2012 on the subject of integrity, the Spirit of God gave me the following message below on integrity of heart and the accompanying 12 principles I will hereafter put in print and impart to you.

I was greatly blessed by the summer Olympics in London 2012, during which I saw world class athletes who had overcome great adversity as children. Oscar Pistorius, a sprinter from South Africa, a double amputee, was told by his mother growing up to "get dressed and put your legs on" and was given no opportunity thereafter to complain. Oscar's mother, as the sports commentator told the story, would tell Oscar and his brother, "Get dressed and put your shoes on" to his brother who had legs – and "put your legs on" to Oscar who had need of legs to enable him to function in life as other children.

Such a motherly strength and fortitude of character deposited into Oscar the prerequisite disposition, DNA and perseverance in character to propel him forward in life and enable him to believe in his abilities. The sprinter from South Africa inspired the world with his athleticism and heart as he ran in the London Games.

Whenever you feel overwhelmed and overcome by your circumstances, remember Oscar Pistorius and keep things in perspective.

Sometimes when I feel sorry for myself or feel stressed out by reason of the many challenges of life, I get a quick wake-up call from God when I drive to the end of my street and see two young adults in wheelchairs outside who live at the end of my street. Immediately I start thanking God for all my blessings and stop inwardly complaining.

As long as the focus is on ourselves, we will feel incapable and somewhat overwhelmed by the many challenges of life. However when we realize God's ability begins when our ability ends, we will look at challenges and struggles as opportunities for God to show up and show Himself strong in our lives and on our behalf.

Therefore cultivating a divine relationship with our Creator is a part of being an overcomer, keeping a pure heart and maintaining the right perspective in all things.

1.   HEART

Integrity begins with the heart.

How open is your heart to people who don't LOOK like you? Don't TALK like you? Don't THINK like you?

Champions are made often in the furnace of affliction, the crucible of circumstantial pressure and struggles that test the fortitude of our character.

Some of my favorite Olympic athletes (Gabby Douglas, Reese Hoffa and Dannell Leyva) had people who looked at them beyond their skin color and biology to see their heart and potential. The parents of these great athletes were not always the biological parents, but they played a loving and nurturing role to give wings to their dreams and enable them to soar to new heights and levels in life.

Even when we feel fatherless, without loving parents, or all alone in life; there is a God, a heavenly Father up above looking down on us with love. My three favorite Olympic athletes had the priceless treasure of experiencing a heart connection with loving, nurturing parents who were committed to them and cultivated their greatness long before we ever knew their names or saw them compete on a world stage.

Thus alongside these athletes their parents (be they adopted parents, proxy parents, host parents for a brief homestay, or heartfelt encouragers of their dreams) also rose to greatness to share in the Olympic dream and victories of these shining stars.

Reese Hoffa was an orphan until his loving mother adopted him. Reese, a shot put thrower in the Olympics, said of his mother that she brought him good luck. Reese won a bronze medal in the London Games.

Olympic gymnast Gabby Douglas at 14 left her family in Virginia Beach (and the gym where she experienced racism) to train in Des Moines, Iowa with Chinese coach Liang Chow. To do so, Gabby needed a place to live and family to take her in. Gabby's first host family didn't work out, but the Parton family (which already had 4 girls of their own) took Gabby in saying, "As long as Gabby is living under our roof, she will be treated as our own daughter." Because of such love and integrity of heart, Gabby Douglas won the gold medal in the women's all-around gymnast competition.

Dannell Leyva's stepfather and coach Yin Alvarez and mother Maria Gonzalez were members of Cuba's national gymnastics team. Dannell's mother escaped Cuba and moved to Miami when Dannell was a year old. Dannell's stepfather Yin Alvarez escaped Cuba by swimming across the Rio Grande to the United States while his team was competing in Mexico. Today Dannell's mom and stepfather run a gym in Miami.

As I watched the heartfelt affection of Dannell's stepfather and the way he lavished praise and love on his stepson, I immediately was brought to remembrance of my own traumatic and troublesome childhood.

My mom was a drug addict and alcoholic who was never around – either at a bar getting drug, out chasing another man, in jail for substance abuse, a rehab to try to get her life back on track, or a mental war after she fried her brain on drugs and alcohol.

My stepmother was a bit cold and distant at times during my younger years, using me often as a house slave to do her dirty work in the yard and at home. To her credit she was a source of stability and a good provider, undoubtedly a step up from my biological mother. Yet back in those days my stepmother was quick to love and show affection to my younger brother, her biological son, and slow to give the same to me.

Hence I experienced racism and prejudice within my own home as a child growing up. We bicker about racism in politics, government, society and church; but the sad reality is often in our own homes stepchildren are treated as rejects and outcasts who we care less for.

Thankfully however God Almighty embraces those others reject and rescues their lives from destruction. For this reason God says pure religion is to comfort the widows and orphans in their affliction (James 1:27). God loves loners and those who are rejected, realizing they within them have the seeds of greatness, which if watered with a bit of love and life-giving inspiration can flourish greatly and be mighty in the earth to the glory of God!

Experiencing such deep hurt and rejection as a child at the hands of a wayward mother and stepmother who saw me more as an obligation than a son caused me to draw near to God as a friend. Thankfully my father and grandfathers were wonderful men who enabled me to easily embrace the concept as God being a loving heavenly Father.

Pop-Pop, my maternal grandfather, was the best grandpa a boy could ask for. He never missed any of my baseball games and always made time to play with me every weekend whether it was going bowling or to a ballgame. Pop-Pop was my very best friend in life.

Although Pop-Pop was a U.S. Army retired Lt. Colonel, he was a very happy-go-lucky guy and gentleman with a great sense of humor. Pop-Pop was loved by everybody in the community, church and wherever he went.

Even strangers and waitresses at restaurants easily took a shine to Pop-Pop as he was truly a people person, approachable and relatable.

My father, Paul Sr. is also very fun to be around, he too having a great sense of humor. My dad has a different set of skills, he being a former home builder and licensed real estate broker and appraiser. My dad taught me how to pitch and play baseball, along with so many other things pertaining to work, life and survival.

Although it was a different type of relationship than with my grandfather, my father is a very special man who God used to train and groom me for greatness in a unique way. My dad had me attend church, study spirituality, listen to motivational lectures, learn real estate, pursue a university degree and many other things that greatly helped my personal development.

Even when my father spanked me for bringing home a D in science in 6th grade (although he nor my school teacher step-mother never sat down with me before or after to teach me how to study - LOL), it worked toward my betterment to put the fear of God in me (or at least of my dad's temper and belt) to compel me to take school more seriously.

As a result the next science test I had, I studied earnestly and scored 100% both on locating all the bones of the body on a blank diagram and spelling them correctly. Incidentally, I was awarded at the end of the year as the most improved student by my teacher.

To my surprise to this day I still have not taken an exam as difficult as that test I took in 6th grade with a blank diagram asking me to name the bones of the body and spell them correctly. Thankfully I taught myself the bones (and years later the muscles) when going on to become a personal fitness trainer. Thus the skill set I mastered as early as 6th grade served me well in adulthood.

As for the motivational lectures my dad had me listen to (rather than the radio), well, today I am a worldwide motivational speaker who has touched 70 countries by the grace of God. To God be the glory, as without His divine protection and supernatural power on my life, I'd most likely be dead considering the many infirmities I had while living overseas and the perilous war-torn countries wherein I journeyed and could have had my life cut short.

So you see and can learn from these Olympic champion's life stories and my own, success has many fathers and mothers, but failure is always an orphan. President John F. Kennedy indeed said this accurately and it is a timeless truth.

The good news and message to take away from the Olympians I admire is even when your parents seem distant and your mentors are nowhere to be found, God can be your friend and provide for you people who genuinely care and take a wholehearted interest in you.

Everyone has a role to play in our lives if we will but keep our eyes and ears open to listen and learn. Each one no matter how small should be cherished and celebrated. I thank God for my step-mother being a stable figure in my life and a consistent provider. She was certainly a step up from my biological mother who essentially abandoned me to pursue pleasure, the latter of which was her own demise.

As for my beloved step-mother, I today call her mother and our relationship has greatly improved; we both being much more kindhearted and affectionate toward one another. Like my dad, my mom has an ace personality, and we always have a lot of fun when we are together. Mom has been real sweet and welcoming of her first grandchild too, which we look forward to welcoming into the world around the last week of August, 2013.

I thank God for my Nana, my beloved maternal grandmother who loved me like a mother (the best mother I ever had as a boy) and taught me how to pray. Nana a former house maid before she married Pop-Pop was a humble Slovakian woman from Natrona Heights outside of Pittsburgh, Pennsylvania. She was sweet, sincere and soft spoken.

Nana rarely smiled in photographs as she had experienced great pain throughout her life. Nana's father died when she was only 3 years of age and her stepfather didn't last much longer thereafter. As a mother, Nana was tormented by trying to raise a rebellious teenager who grew up in the age of drug and alcohol experimentation. Unlike most kids who grow out of such frivolous activities, my mother was ensnared and never found her way out.

My mom was adopted and struggled with rejection. If only she could have just believed and received all the love we had for her, rather than listening to her own inner lies and thoughts about being rejected. Truly our self-worth, self-evaluation and identity (or the lack thereof) positively effects or dwarfs our destiny.

I certainly had ample opportunity to struggle with the same feelings of rejection given my troubled relationship with my mom and stepmother. Yet by God's grace I embraced a higher perspective and vision of myself and for my life. When you know you are created in God's image, any lesser images people have of you (even if they are in your own family) are miniscule and meaningless in the light of God's glory!

As movie producer and comedian Tyler Perry recently told Piers Morgan during an interview, "Our parents also have stories." Tyler had a father who was abusive toward him. Tyler forgave his father and came to the realization that he too was abused to some extent and perpetuated his pain, causing the generational curse to continue.

Thankfully however when we become more self-aware, humble and are apt to listen we can learn the life lessons God is trying to teach us and avoid the pitfalls and stumbling blocks that so easily and readily can snare our families and trip many of us up. Rise up and break the generational curses of old to declare and enter newness of life in Jesus Christ!

When we forgive, we live lighter and enable others to do likewise without the burden and heavy weight of guilt and shame. God is love (1John 4:16). Love covers a multitude of sins (Proverbs 10:12).

Although forgiving those who have wronged us may not always be easy, nor feel like something we want to do, when we decide to do so regardless of what we feel; somehow supernaturally by way of our godly decision we inwardly begin to heal.

God hears and responds to our decisions knowing that the feelings may not always be there. Nevertheless God honors and sees our actions, along with which He will show up to help us every step of the way and uphold us when we are weak to keep us from falling.

So the next time you feel inclined to judge someone before taking the time to listen to their life story, feel their pain and hear their heart; ask yourself what about them you don't know. Take time to feel before you think to label and look down upon others.

Think of yourself as an orphan, a stranger in a foreign country; and do unto others as you would have them do unto you. Love more and live better!

Nevertheless if you find yourself alone, know that even when your father and mother forsake you God will embrace, make you His own and care for you! (Psalm 27:10) God is a father to the fatherless, a mother to the motherless and a Friend that sticks closer than a brother (Proverbs 18:24).

Whenever you find yourself in need, stop, look up and cry out to big Daddy up above to hug, love, comfort, provide for and lead you.

Integrity begins with the heart. Heart and passion lifts everyone. As a sophomore Tim Tebow looked over to his coach Urban Meyer leading the University of Florida football team and asked to play. Tebow told coach: "It's all heart!" Once Tebow got on the gridiron, as a sophomore he won a Heisman Trophy and led the Florida Gators to a national championship.

There is nothing you cannot do when you put your mind and heart into it! Urban Meyer, when asked as to the secret of their success, said of his Florida Gator team: "They are heavily invested."

Therefore the first thing you must invest in any relationship or endeavor to see success is HEART.

2. RESPECT

As the soldiers in the military know, their commanders give you only three ways to respond: "Yes sir. No sir. No excuse sir."

This spirit and heart embodies respect for the chain of command and our country. Respectfully honoring and submitting to authority is life-changing.

When soldiers fail to submit to authority and resist doing so, they will find themselves being severely and swiftly punished. Some are made to work the entire weekend doing chores like cleaning the kitchen, bathrooms and doing other tasks.

Some punishment comes in the form of more pushups and rigorous exercise (in addition to what has already been required).

Soon before long soldiers learn they must show respect lest they be disrespected and made to endure more harsh punishment. As in society and the military, you don't break the law, the law breaks you.

One old song simply and repeatedly says, "I fought the law and the law one." That is a timeless message every generation must learn.

If there is one thing that impressed me the most about the U.S. Army General, Colonels, officers, leaders and staff at TACOM's control center in Michigan when I spoke there on suicide prevention in 2012 it was their deep respect for and commitment to one another.

At the time of writing this book, my wife is pregnant with our first child. Yet we have already had a conversation about what we shall do when our children become teenagers. I told my wife, if our kids get too big for their britches and think they don't have to obey us during their teenage years, I will send them to a boarding / military like school to teach them respect and discipline.

I refuse to have a power struggle in my home and endure much of what American parents subject themselves to because of their kids lack of respect for authority.

It is important to teach your children, employees and students (if you are an educator) respect early on lest they run all over you. Family, home, corporate and classroom management all require a foundation of healthy respect (a respect that comes for authority and from the heart realizing that by respecting authority it is ultimately best and good for everybody).

Of course respect is further earned when we lead by example and not just demand it based on our position. Where marriages, families, companies and schools lack respect; there is utter chaos and lack of excellence. Thus there is a lack of purposeful accomplishment and little passion present.

Respect yourself and others. Be true to and respect yourself even when nobody else does. The secret to FSU football coach Bobbie Bowden's success was he taught his football players to love and respect one another. Bobbie knew if he could get his players to love and respect each other, than they would block for each other and win games.

Colliding with authority initially may hurt and be painful, but if embraced, honored and submitted to; authority will be the best thing that ever happened to you. Because the authority you submit to, you then can have a degree of by reason of your obedience.

When you submit to the law of the land, you too as a citizen can make an arrest in your community, when something illegal is occurring in your midst. A citizen's arrest is not something we think of, but if you consult you state penal code, you will indeed see it does in fact exist.

Therefore when a Police Officer pulls you over for speeding or having a light on your car out, entreat and engage the officer respectfully in your greeting and conversation. "Good evening officer! Was I driving too fast?"

By doing so, you will be surprised how often the officer will equally treat you respectfully and sometimes even when you are on the wrong, give you a second chance to do better and not write you up a ticket for the infraction.

In my B.C. days (before Christ) when I was a lot younger, I can honestly say there were at least 5 times I was pulled over by police officers in which I never received a ticket or fine. Why? Because I was respectful and courteous.

Nevertheless even if you receive a ticket (as I once did for jaywalking in Irvine, CA years ago when in Bible College), courteously and politely thank the officer for doing his/her job and don't grow bitter about it.

I know it is hard to believe I got a jaywalking ticket, as walking haphazardly occurs daily throughout New York City, where I also lived. But the standard of orderliness and quality of life in my opinion is significantly better in Irvine than in New York City.

There is a reason why Singapore is so clean and enjoyable to visit. It's called law enforcement. Respect and honor those in authority in your community and country. Your life will be better if you do.

Remember the same law enforcement officer that is giving you a traffic citation one day, may be the very same officer who saves your life the next when someone is trying to rob your house, kill your children, or cause harm in the community.

Therefore respect the position regardless of the person within the uniform (since sometimes people in power can be a bit cocky and disrespectful to citizens – as I have experienced). Therefore even if you don't like your Governor, Mayor, Senator or President; respect the position they hold for the sake of the good of the community and country.

Even when I didn't particularly care for my stepmother growing up, I honored her knowing she was my father's wife and as a result of doing so, today we have a better relationship and I consider her as my own mother.

Keeping a respectful heart and mind will enable you to mature and grow in your manhood/womanhood.

When you show respect for authority, you teach your children to do likewise. The reverse is also true. If you are a negative person with an unruly mouth, it should not be surprising when your kids won't obey their school teachers and talk trash in class when asked to do something. Your children emulate and learn from you! Parents must lead by example at home if they want their children to be harnessed and respectful when they are not around.

Respect yourself and others. Be true to and respect yourself even when nobody else does. Don't judge by appearance, which is merely racism coupled with ignorance. The secret to FSU football coach Bobbie Bowden's success was he taught his football players to love and respect one another. Bobbie knew if he could get his players to love and respect each other, than they would block for each other and win games.

When you behave honorably and show respect for authority (even when you may disagree with them), you set yourself up to find favor and win big in life.

3.   BELIEVE

Believe in yourself even when nobody else does... and don't get bitter because others don't believe in you.

Trust is earned and confidence built over time as you prove yourself. Proving yourself is never quick and easy. Neither can you prove yourself by being overly concerned and fixated on what others say about you.

As one Pastor once said, "People will always talk about you. Even when you are dead and in a casket at the funeral home, they will be talking and saying, 'They didn't do the makeup quite right on her.'"

Therefore let people keep on talking, but you keep on working and walking. Don't let your ears be garbage cans, neither people's pitiful and pathetic attitudes deflate you. Never be dwarfed or diminished by belittling attitudes of others. Refuse to shrink down to the size others see of you. Live large and in charge regardless of their erroneous and limiting beliefs.

Eventually the truth will outlive a lie and God will show up, show off and show Himself strong on your behalf as you remain faithful, pure in heart, and keep going forward doing that which you know to be right in God's sight.

God will provide for (Philippians 4:19), fight for (Exodus 14:25) and defend His kids (Psalm 18). You therefore can rest and live happily knowing God will protect you (Psalm 91) and fight your battles against your accusers (Revelation 12:10).

Satan is known in the Bible as the accuser, that is his job description – to be a liar and accuser (John 8:44; Revelation 12:10) by which the devil comes to kill, steal and destroy people

(John 10:10). Your job however is not to give ear to noisy negatives, neither lies from the pit of hell, but firmly be established and rooted and grounded in the love of the Lord of life and be renewed in the spirit of your mind by the truth of God's Word (by which the earth itself is upheld – Hebrews 11:3; 1:3).

Let the noisy negatives and your doubting critics motivate you to be better. Your haters are your best motivators!

Connect with and hold on to your purpose because it will keep you and help direct your life when you go through difficult times and challenges. When I was hit by a drunk driver and my car totaled, it was a traumatic and trying time for me. Not only was I without transportation and forced to use a rental car, but simultaneously I was embarking upon a new job as a high-school teacher. All the while, I also was battling my evil insurance company who was trying to "low-ball" me and provide a fraudulent valuation of my car, 20% under the true market value for the vehicle (a typical occurrence sadly in the insurance industry).

Upon contacting the State of Florida Department of Financial Services and Insurance Regulation to file a formal complaint against my insurer, I was surprised to see how quickly my insurance company responded. Within 24 hours of the formal complaint being filed, my insurance company realized it wasn't dealing with a rookie but a seasoned negotiator and someone who knew how to fight and battle against fraud.

Unfortunately the opposite is typically true with many good people who trust insurance companies to whom they pay monthly premiums for years to do right by them when they have a car accident. Hence insurance companies often low-ball consumers and concoct fraudulent valuations based on "comparable" vehicles that have been leased and in car accidents. Until doing some fact checking, I too nearly swallowed the lies of my insurer.

However upon buying the VIN reports of every vehicle on the insurance company's subcontractor's report claiming to fairly value my vehicle, I discovered the bogus numbers and unfair "comparables" being used. Thus my insurer moved swiftly to remedy the wrong lest they be slapped with treble damages and be made to pay me 3 times the amount I was owed. Therefore I was paid the full and fair market value of my totaled vehicle, but not before battling them with fierce intensity.

When you have confidence and boldness (the true sign you genuinely believe in yourself) you can stand up to anyone, any organization, association, nation, etc. without intimidation. Even more so when you have God on your side and have done your homework to know the heart and mind of God via His Word and thoroughly investigated the facts relevant to your case, present situation, and circumstance. My investigation and thorough preparation paid off when battling my insurance company.

Therefore luck is nothing more than the meeting of opportunity and preparedness. Unfortunately many people are a bit lazy and are not given to adequate preparation. Many people would rather complain and cultivate a sense of entitlement as they lazily watch TV. Yet God doesn't bless lazy hands and moving mouths. God blesses diligent people with vision and direction who live purposefully every moment of their days.

Never be dismayed by the naysayers. Stay focused. Live with heavenly vision and boldly take dominion rather than discussing mediocre opinions (most of which are like armpits and stink).

Remain true to your authentic to God self and wholeheartedly give yourself to and abide in your calling. Cultivate your garden, whatever it is God has graced you with to do, and consider anyone and anything pulling you elsewhere a distraction. Be true to yourself, abide in your calling, work diligently continually going forward, and rejoice every step of the way as you do!

4.   AUTHENTICITY AND COMMITMENT

Be true and commit to be yourself.

Get a vision for your life, commit to it and put feet to your faith.

Stacy Ann Ferguson was afraid to be true to herself and leave the band Wild Orchid, which she didn't quite jell with. Upon leaving the band Stacy felt lost and became a meth addict.

Yet when Stacy stopped agonizing over her identity and committed to being true to herself and honoring her gift and uniqueness despite the feelings of others; it was then Stacy got off drugs and became Ferggie the lead singer for the hugely successful Black Eyed Peas.

In her time of struggle, Ferggie (the now famous singer) became a drug addict when she was agonizing over trying to be someone she was not to try to fit the mold of a band she previously performed in (or perhaps the desires of others for her life). As I watched the interview with Oprah, I was amazed to see such a transformation and progression into womanhood.

Obviously few singers are a moral compass for their generation, but nevertheless we can learn something from everybody if we will look, listen and mine the hidden treasures among the muck and mire.

Ferggie like many was a young lady trying to find herself and her place in this world. We all are continually evolving, growing, learning, and gradually maturing. Where we start is not as important as where we end up. Therefore we should not judge others based on our preferences and personal tastes – be it music, movies, political ideology, spirituality, etc.

We are all an ongoing work in progress. Moreover God Almighty can come crashing down any day of the week and totally interrupt anyone He chooses and get their attention.

Likewise God can opt to patiently interact with people, gently put signs in their path and send various messengers in their way to communicate vital lifesaving truths to them.

How God deals with humanity is never formulaic but always individualized within the context of His divine plan for each person. God is not a cookie cutter, but rather the author of life and Perfecter of mankind.

How God deals with human beings is His business. Our job is to love unconditionally and honor God in people, regardless of how they choose to express themselves and relate to society. We all come from different backgrounds and understandably are taking uniquely different journeys quite frequently. Where there be some commonality we together can rejoice, but equally we should learn to rejoice in our differences and wholeheartedly learn from them.

Upon leaving, overcoming substance abuse and reconnecting with her true authentic self; Ferggie found mega-success in the Black Eyed Peas.

Don't judge others by appearance. It's easy to judge people and situations based on appearance, but appearances can be deceiving. Therefore be gracious and believe the best about others and yourself, knowing that in an atmosphere of love and acceptance we all do better.

When Ferggie stopped lying to herself and trying to be who she was not, she began to more freely express herself and live fearlessly. It was then her audience began to connect with her, enjoy her music and her influence was enlarged to a global scale.

Personalizing this message to you, what is it about you that you pull back on, try to repackage and rework to be more likeable? How have you denied your true to God authentic self?

What can you do (or give place to) so as to allow yourself more freedom to simply BE –
BE yourself, BE happy, BE present in the moment, BE spontaneous, BE creative, BE crazy, BE
fun, BE silent without getting nervous about what others think, BE able to dance without fear of
the opinions of others, BE free to try new things without feeling obligated to explain yourself,
BE daring to try something fresh and out of the ordinary, BE willing to break the mold and
surprise people, BE unapologetic about being true to yourself and offending people.

Jesus said, "Blessed are you who are not offended in Me' (Matthew 11:6). Thus Jesus
was offensive and not always politically correct. Jesus told the Pharisees who hid behind their
religious pretense, "Your father is the devil" (John 8:44). Jesus rebuked one of His favorite
disciples Peter calling him Satan and an offense to the work of God (Matthew 16:23). The irony
is shortly before this sharp rebuke, Jesus told Peter how blessed he was for discovering and
grasping the revelation that Christ was the Savior of the world (Matthew 16:17).

Nevertheless Jesus was true to Himself and unafraid about how people responded to Him,
including those such as His very own disciples who He held near and dear. Jesus wasn't afraid to
lose it all to remain true to Himself.

I heard actor and singer Jamie Foxx tell Oprah something similar in an interview,
wherein he admitted to taking some very big risks throughout his career; which he identified
would either make or break him.

Taking risks doesn't come easy for some people. Why? Because they don't believe in
themselves. They don't believe in God in them and God's hand upon their lives. Thus they live
in timidity, always second-guessing themselves and therefore living in captivity.

To truly be free you have to give place to who you truly are without apology. If people don't like, accept, embrace, or celebrate you that is THEIR PROBLEM not yours.

Therefore spread your wings like an eagle and prepare to soar when the winds of God blow. Open your heart and let the rivers of the Spirit flow. Let God take you from low self-esteem and feeling like a zero into transforming you into a giant killer and mighty hero! Bury false humility and start to live freely so you can truly be happy!

Commit and put feet to your faith.

Get a vision for your life and put one foot in front of the other daily to journey toward it. Don't wait for your ship to come in. Swim out to it as sea if you have to. As you swim and go deeper daily, your fears will fall off of you, be forever drowned and be no more.

Sometimes as you walk by faith and not by sight (2Corinthians 5:7), you have to be willing to launch out into the deep, to walk on water, and even fake it until you make it as you trust God to uphold you and give you success.

God has given us in His Word the formula for great success: meditating upon His word of faith day and night, speaking according thereto, and putting feet to our faith and traveling thereto (Joshua 1:8).

Journeying to your destiny can be painful, turbulent and test you in a multiplicity of ways. When I committed and decided to go to Bible College in southern California, I had to leave the comfort of living with my grandparents where all of my needs were provided for and I didn't have a worry in the world.

I had nobody in Orange County (OC), California – not a friend, not an acquaintance and no family members. I had a distant uncle in Los Angeles who I'd never met, but he was nowhere near Orange County where I would be attending Bible College. Furthermore Orange County was full of millionaires and very expensive for me compared to the cost of living in Orlando, Florida (also Orange County) where I grew up.

Nevertheless I was willing to pay the price, risk it all and "launch out into the deep" (Luke 5:4) to make it happen. Although I knew no one in southern California, I knew a God in heaven who held the world in His hands and would make a way for me.

With only a phone number for a potential roommate (and he never answered his telephone to take my phone calls), I left Orlando en route to John Wayne airport in Orange County. Even upon arrival in OC, I still had nobody, nor a place to stay.

I had given my truck to my best friend in Orlando, anticipating living in California and not needing it. Upon arriving at John Wayne airport, I phoned my grandfather in Orlando, gave him Jeff's number (the prospective roommate who never answered his phone), and asked him to call on my behalf and inform Jeff I was at the airport waiting for him to phone me back at the given number.

Looking back in retrospect and considering all of this today, I cannot but laugh and cringe in fear thinking I did all of this. I had less than $1,000 in my pocket, about $750, most of which would pay for half of my annual tuition (that having come from selling nearly 40,000 baseball cards, my prized collection from my entire childhood). It greatly hurt to do so, but I was believing God for great things and an anointing from heaven to blast through and revive the nations of the world.

God did not disappoint. Although I slept on the floor for 2 years, while sharing a small bedroom in an apartment (two apartments over a two year timeframe), I graduated with good marks and got an impartation, divine revelation and Holy Ghost supernatural wisdom whereby I have since been able to touch 70 nations and am just getting started. Truly the best is yet to come as we continue to believe and go forward with childlike faith.

When Jeff drove to pick me up at John Wayne airport that summer evening in 1992, his prayers were answered. Jeff had been laying on his couch depressed asking God for a roommate. Yet he didn't have the heart to even get off the couch and pick up the ringing phone. Thankfully when he heard my sweet Pop-Pop's voice on the answer machine, Jeff got up.

Something, somewhere, somehow, some way, through someone you are going to be provoked, inspired, ignited and uplifted. When the stirring of the Holy Spirit invades your life and awakens your heart RESPOND, GET UP, MOVE and don't sit still.

Take immediate action! This is what Philip did when he heard the voice of the Holy Spirit, he ran to fulfill, obey and give way to the working of the miracles of God (Acts 8:29-30). So to must you! You must do you part and cooperate and work with God. Do your part and God will assuredly do His. Remember God will not do it all, you must do your part and co-labor with God in the process.

God likes to work miracles, but our Creator works with humanity. Give God something to work with! Do your part. Use your gifts, talents and abilities. Stop doubting! Get up and do something different! Go somewhere new! Shake some hands. Interact with new people.

Change your mindset and get rid of stinking thinking that confines and keeps you stuck in cramped quarters and small spaces. Enlarge your heart by believing and you will enlarge your life to start receiving countless miracles, signs, wonders and blessings from God.

A dream is not enough, you must daily do something to fulfill your dreams and make them a living reality. A dream without daily discipline and effort is merely a fantasy.

Fantasia is the meeting place of the masses and marketplace of entrepreneurs. Facebook capitalized on creating a meeting place in cyberspace to acquaint people with idle time on their hands. Walt Disney capitalized on the human tendency and propensity to gravitate to fantasy over reality as a means of escape, which he through motion pictures and movies made a fortune producing and selling.

Disney had a vision and dream. Disney was childlike and bold in his faith, being a doer and huge risk taker. Few people know Walt Disney went bankrupt three times pursuing his dream. Before Disney died, while Epcot (at Walt Disney World was under construction) an employee said to him, "What a pity Mr. Disney that you will never see Epcot full constructed before you die."

Disney chuckled and replied, "Oh yes I have! I envisioned and saw Epcot's completion long ago. For without me Epcot never would be."

What you see you can build. What you see you can do. If you can see it, you can have it. The inner visions you get are not only for your benefit, but God sent to motivate you to take action, initiative and bring them to full fruition in the earth!

Too many of us are living in fantasy, not giving place to our inner reality, which ultimately could manifest and truly be if we'd only believe and dare to build it. As in the film *The Field of Dreams*, we must build it before people will come.

Too often we are looking for praise when we haven't yet embarked to do something new in silence without applause. Unless you can take action alone, when nobody knows who you are, or cares to applaud you; then your dreams will never take place and become a reality.

Everything big begins with something small. Babies are nurtured and hid in the womb nine and a half months before coming forth into the world. Long before being impregnated, mothers go on dates and arouse a twinkle in their man's eye. Wedding bells usually precede childbearing.

Most of us enjoy a good wedding celebration, but few know the extent and intricacies involved in planning and thoroughly preparing for a wedding. There are invitations to buy, write, stamp and mail. There are dinners to prepare and serve. There is a venue that needs to be rented and decorated. There are tuxedos and dresses that need to be bought. The bride's hair needs to be done and her gown held as she walks down the aisle.

These seemingly small details are usually overlooked by the crowd who just comes to celebrate, have a good meal, give a gift and drive home afterward.

Yet planning and preparing a memorable wedding takes months and months of work beforehand. Your dream and lifelong purpose will be no different. Nobody can do and live it for you.

As every pregnant woman knows, there may be a momentary celebration at the announcement of a baby to be in the future. But the mother alone will be doing the pushing. You likewise must carry your own dream like a pregnant mother with child.

You alone must do your own homework, stay encouraged, strategically plan, purpose, persevere, go forward when you feel exhausted and like you want to quit, and silence the noisy negatives coming from relatives and less than believing "friends" who doubt your abilities.

Integrity of heart is about you, what you cultivate within and how you master your moods and mindsets. Mindsets are like frequencies and channels on a radio; they can be changed and the volume adjusted accordingly.

How loud and with what intensity you hear and lock into your purpose is up to you. The level of passion and persistence you harness and go forth in must be decided upon only by you. Self-mastery is a daily discipline and your personal pace may vary day to day.

Your diet (physically, spiritually, mentally and emotionally) must be predetermined and not be haphazard. To have mental stamina and consistency, you need to hear from and associate with people who have attained the same and can impart this spirit and mental fitness to you. Such impartation is not necessarily transferred via instruction, but more so through observation and meaningful communication. This communication can be conveyed via one's temperament, demeanor, disposition, attitude, the intensity of their responses to certain stimuli, the audacity with which they push back on noisy negatives and doubt.

Doubting is being double-minded, which gives birth to instability in all your ways (James 1:8). Thus the holy Scriptures tell us, 'he who doubts is damned' (Romans 14:27). In other words, if you are doubtful, double-minded, second guessing yourself, aroused by mental masturbation, contained by hesitation, vacillation and imprisoned by intimidation; then you are shipwreck and incapable of going forward and accomplishing anything.

Therefore you must get rid of paralysis by excessive analysis. Simply believe and take action on that which you know to do, utilizing your gifts, talents and abilities to the full.

Integrity of heart means you wholeheartedly devote and give yourself to something greater than yourself and step into it daily in some small way until the faithfulness of your daily routine manifests into something greater. As you continually and daily step into greatness and the greater illumination and light that it brings, you will gain new perspective, illumination and insight on your journey to progress further and process yourself as a person always evolving, growing and going.

Go the extra mile, because few do. Most people are lazy and aren't willing to pay the price. When you go the extra mile, you will discover there is a lot of room at the top to enjoy the view, scenery and blessings of success.

5. MATURITY AND MOTIVES

A me, myself and I attitude never makes it in relationships, sports, business and the real world. Situations and circumstances will always eventually reveal and grind down your motives.

If you are all about yourself, seeking only what is best for you, without considering the feelings and needs of others, you won't do well in life. Being self-centered always prolongs and delays your success, because success requires a multiplicity of people and cooperation to make it happen.

TEAM simply means together everyone accomplishes more. Getting people to work together as a team however is no easy task. You don't have to look far for examples of teamwork or the lack thereof. Many professional sports teams have star players, but cannot win championships. The missing ingredient is always teamwork.

FSU legendary coach Bobbie Bowden won more college football games than most ever dreamed of winning. When I watched a documentary on Bowden and his coaching secrets, Bobbie surprised me when he revealed one of his underlying foundational pillars to his success.

"I teach my players to love one another." I thought to myself, "Really? This is the secret to a football coach's success?"

Bobbie continued, "If players don't love one another, they won't block for one another. If I can teach my boys to love one another, they will block for one another and we will win football games." (I realize I mentioned Coach Bowden earlier within the chapter on RESPECT, but the same selfless attitude here reveals MATURITY of character – a quality found within winners!)

Simple, profound and proven principles from a veteran and very successful football coach. Love! This word is often easily said, but rarely done (as indicative by the 50% divorce rate in the western world and our country). As a minister who sometimes officiates weddings – itietheknot.com – this truly concerns me.

I don't have to look far to see the many professions of love when couples get married, but once they begin living together, paying bills, caring for kids, washing dishes, doing laundry, and maintaining the yard; what was said to be LOVE somehow begins to diminish and disappear.

Perhaps when circumstantial challenges and pressures collide with LOVE and the battles of LIFE show up, what was previously called LOVE is later revealed to only be LUST out of convenience merely pursuing momentary pleasure not a lifelong commitment requiring selflessness.

Perhaps this is why Jesus scratched all the other commandments from the Old Testament given by Moses and transcended them simply by commanding His disciples and followers to love God and love their neighbor as themselves.

When you love people, you won't steal from them, lie about them, falsely accuse them, belittle them, make a mockery of them, sabotage their success, be envious, or hate them in your heart.

Life's circumstances have a way of not only revealing to you your motives, but further grinding them down. Life will give you ample opportunity to come face to face with yourself and choose whether or not you will remain the same and repeat the old patterns or embrace change.

College football coach Charlie Strong joined the University of Florida coaching staff as a graduate assistant in 1984. Years later Strong was hired as defensive coordinator for the Florida Gators before the beginning of the 2003 season.

'When the University of Florida's head coach Ron Zook was fired midway through the Gators' 2004 season, but continued to coach until the bowl game; Strong served as interim coach of the Gators for one game, the December 2004 Peach Bowl. Florida lost the game, 27–10, to the Miami Hurricanes. Florida credits the regular season to Zook and the Peach Bowl to Strong. When Urban Meyer was hired as Florida's head coach, Strong was the only assistant coach retained from Zook's staff.'

'In a January 2009 interview with the *Orlando Sentinel*, Strong expressed his belief that race played a large part in the reason that he hadn't been offered a head coaching job at that point. Strong, whose wife is white, especially cited prospective employers' discomfort with his interracial relationship. Florida ended up hiring Utah's Urban Meyer, who would lead Florida to two national titles' and became 'the coach at the top of every programs wish list.'

Charlie 'Strong became the 21st head football coach at the University of Louisville on December 9, 2009. In a telephone interview that day with ESPN.com columnist Pat Forde, former Indianapolis Colts head coach Tony Dungy, himself African American, said of Strong, "When they see what he can do, you're probably going to have a lot of people disappointed they didn't hire him sooner."

Strong led Louisville to a victory in the 2013 Sugar Bowl over University of Florida by a final score of 33-23.' [http://en.wikipedia.org/wiki/Charlie_Strong]

The mistake the University of Florida made is not hiring Charlie Strong and promoting from within their coaching staff. When Louisville triumphed over the Florida Gators on national television at the Sugar Bowl, justice finally came for Charlie Strong and the victory was sweet. Nevertheless when asked about the University of Florida, Strong responded with class stating that he was thankful for his time at UF and had great respect for the their athletic program.

This scenario repeats itself often in sports and the business world, where CEOs and executives are hired from afar, while the guy who has been working his tail off for years gets passed by and goes unnoticed. Eventually when the overlooked employee finally gets his day to lead the organization and shine, all the higher-ups are surprised. Yet the everyday people down below slaving away who nobody sees or recognizes; they already knew for years who the real leader was.

It's behooves us to listen more to the people in our organization who consistently fulfill small roles, because they too have eyes and ears and can help us discern things occurring when we are not around.

As for grinding down our motives and maturing our character; circumstances and situational scenarios will do just that. Basketball star Lebron James could not win a championship at Cleveland (or so he thought), so he became a free agent and moved to Miami to play for the Heat. After a national press conference (ridiculous and unheard of for a professional athlete merely changing franchises) and much hoopla, Lebron began playing for the Miami Heat.

But Lebron's first year in Miami came up short, as the Heat lost the national championship. Not being a basketball fan (given that I'm under 6 feet in height and never played much myself) I didn't follow much of the season and frankly was turned off by all the hype when Lebron did move to Florida (my home state).

Nevertheless for some reason I watched the championships in year 2 of Lebron playing for the Heat at Miami and was happy I did. The best moment after Miami won the championship was during the interview with Lebron when the commentator conducting the interview asked Lebron, "Lebron, what made the difference for you between year 1 and 2 with Miami?"

Lebron replied (as I recall), "Last year I played with hate. I felt like a had to prove myself. This year I played with love, honored my teammates, recognized I couldn't do it alone and we need each other and we won."

Wise words from a true champion who experienced the grinding down of his pride, ego, motives and simultaneously the shaping of his manhood and athleticism so as to lead his team to victory.

Chris Bosh, also another star player from the Miami Heat, moved from Toronto, where he was the face of his franchise to play second fiddle to Lebron in Miami. Before Lebron and Bosh moved to Miami, Dwayne Wade led the Heat to a championship and was the team's star player. Thus bringing three hugely successful stars together on the same team and basketball court and asking them to cooperatively play together, share the glory, put the team first before themselves individually was a challenging endeavor which could not be accomplished overnight.

Yet through faith, patience, perseverance and hard work the Miami Heat led by coach Erik Spoelstra, conquered the obstacles, purged their souls of selfishness, and together as a team formed in the crucible of circumstances marvelously overcame to win an NBA championship.

Erik Spoelstra is the first Asian American head coach to win an NBA championship. Spoelstra served under legendary hall of fame basketball coach Pat Riley. From 2001 to 2008, Spoelstra fulfilled the role of assistant coach and director of scouting for the Heat.

'Spoelstra joined the Heat staff in 1995 as the team's video coordinator after his father called Chris Wallace, then the director of player personnel for the Heat. After two years, Spoelstra was named assistant coach/video coordinator, then promoted to assistant coach/advance scout in 1999. Spoelstra became the assistant coach/director of scouting in 2001. Spoelstra was cited by *Sports Illustrated* (May 30, 2005) for honing star guard Dwyane Wade's "shooting balance and smoothing out his release after the Flash's return from the Athens Olympics."

Spoelstra was an assistant coach with the Miami Heat when they won the 2006 NBA Finals by defeating the Dallas Mavericks, overcoming a 0–2 deficit.

In April 2008, Spoelstra was named successor to Pat Riley as head coach of the Miami Heat. In naming Spoelstra as head coach, Riley said: "This game is now about younger coaches who are technologically skilled, innovative, and bring fresh new ideas. That's what we feel we are getting with Erik Spoelstra. He's a man that was born to coach." Riley also noted: "A lot of players want the discipline; they will play [hard] for Spoelstra, because they respect him."

Spoelstra coached the Heat to the NBA Finals in 2011 where they lost 4–2 against the Dallas Mavericks. On December 16, 2011, he received a contract extension. On June 21, 2012, Spoelstra's Heat won the NBA Finals against the Oklahoma City Thunder 4-1.' [http://en.wikipedia.org/wiki/Erik_Spoelstra]

The journey of our lives take many twists and turns, which reveal to us our many strengths and weaknesses. As we remain open to personal improvement, correction and instruction; we can continually grow and mature. Resisting opportunities to improve yourself is a sign of insecurity and immaturity.

Motives are easily discerned and felt when you interact with people. If they are not good listeners, cannot honor others, speak with a tone that exudes self-centeredness and self-exaltation; you better beware of them because they are trouble waiting to happen.

A true leader recognizes others. Teddy Bridgewater, quarterback for Louisville was quick to recognize his teammates when being interviewed after winning the Sugar Bowl in 2013. Teddy is probably one of the best quarterback's in college football. Bridgewater's ability to scramble and elude the defense during a blitz, find an open man down field, and throw the ball right in his hands is special.

Unfortunately everyone we deal with in life is not so special. Nevertheless they too can teach us something if we keep our eyes and ears open.

A young neighborhood guy (probably about 17 years of age) came by my house to cut my grass one day. He was trying to persuade me to allow him (and pay him) to regularly cut my grass. I was a bit hesitant as he didn't seem too sharp, but since he only wanted $20 I agreed to allow him to cut my grass and trim my bushes that day.

After going back inside to return to my work (thinking the kid could handle cutting the grass and my bushes without my oversight) it wasn't long before the doorbell rang. "Can I use your clippers?" the kid asked.

"Uh, I thought I was paying you. You're supposed to be a professional and have your own tools. Why do you need to use mine?" Then came a series of excuses, after which I in a bit of pity agreed reluctantly to allow the kid to use my clippers on the condition that next time he bring his own. LOL Next time he brought the neighbor's clippers (and maybe lawnmower as well) to work on my yard.

I'm sure by now you know this kid was more trouble than he was worth and the $20 should have gone to me for enduring all of the drama the kid brought into my life. Certainly my time is more valuable to me than $20 an hour and the aggravation alone wasn't worth dealing with this kid.

Other less than successful lawn guys who briefly worked for me clipped my sprinkler heads and one even scratched his riding lawnmower along the side of my house (which the latter promised to return and repair, but he never did).

I had a repairman my wife found on CraigsList who came to fix my washing machine. He charged me $140 and the machine still didn't work correctly after he left. Six weeks later when the repairman returned, he expected me to pay him another $40 for driving over to the house, $18 to fix another part, and a few more bucks for his labor (around $70 in total).

So the "repairman" milked me for over $200 to "fix" a washing machine, which I could have bought a brand new one for $300 or so. That was a painful lesson and I pray to God the washing machine now works properly for some years, because that whole ordeal was painful.

The repairman was yelling at me in my home telling me how much he expected to be paid on his second repair visit (after not doing a good job the first time). His warranty obviously meant nothing since it didn't last more than a few weeks and thereafter he (unlike Sears or any other reputable appliance company) didn't return for free to fix the machine to work properly. Instead he wanted to charge me a second time and double dip.

Were my wife not pregnant at the time, I would have really laid into this repairman and not given him another penny, but I didn't want to trouble or stress out my wife and baby in the womb. Some things matter more than money. Do yourself a favor and save yourself the hassles and drama by hiring quality people.

You see, when you give someone your word, but fail to follow through; you show to them and yourself that your word is worthless. When your word is worthless, so too is your name and reputation!

Some people in churches wonder why God won't bless them and fulfill His Word promising prosperity in their lives. Often the reason is simply they are not fulfilling the prerequisite conditions to do their part to warrant and attract the blessing of God.

In other words, they are unworthy of the blessing of God because of their own laziness, passivity, and lack of vision. Such people lack direction and often live in indecision. Yet they usually are full and overflowing with excuses as to why they are jobless and unsuccessful.

Truth be told, if you were to ask and interview people who really know unsuccessful people, they would tell you how lazy unsuccessful people are and how often they cannot keep their word.

You see if you cannot keep your word when you say and commit to something, don't think you have the right to hold God to His Word. God Himself says, "Whatever you say in my ears I will do to you" (Numbers 14:28).

Therefore when smooth talkers make empty promises they never plan to deliver, God just steps back, folds His arms, and allows them to come to the end of themselves. Only then can they come to grips with their character flaws and areas within their lives that need to change and be reformed.

Unless you become self-aware and brutally honest with yourself, you can never truly reform your ways and be the man or woman God will bless and honor in society. Successful people are humble, broken, self-aware, thoughtful, mindful and sincere.

Don't kid yourself for a minute and think successful people make it on their gifting alone. On the contrary, star athletes practice hard and are always working on improving their game.

Google the stats on Lebron James and you may be surprised to learn that every year his numbers (rebounds, shooting percentage, successful free throws, defense) are improving. Although he is an NBA champion, the Lebron is still working on his game, improving and building upon the fundamentals.

When we stray from the fundamentals of success and think to take shortcuts, we always trip up and delay our personal and organizational progress. Many are they on Wall Street who are going bankrupt because of shortcuts taken to "get rich" – decisions that in actuality impoverished their companies, squandered assets, trusted crooks, and by trying to make a buck fast rather than protecting the assets on the books, thereby lost it all in a moment.

Cities, states and nations likewise are bankrupt; having squandered public taxpayers' hard earned money. I recently heard on 60 Minutes that the states of Illinois, New Jersey and California are bankrupt (among others in the union).

Integrity demands we think about more than ourselves, lest our self-absorbed and self-centered mentality get us a day in the spotlight we don't want, as we are handcuffed and hauled off to jail with the on looking press, media and TV cameras.

It's better to do the right thing and sleep with peace in your heart at night, than to take shortcuts and trip yourself up only to thereafter become the brunt of everyone's jokes as they make a laughingstock of you.

But people don't see it like this, nor do they fully think things through when they are contemplating fraud. Crooks only see the millions in the movie screens of their minds. They don't see all the heartache and pain caused. They don't see precious grandmas penniless because they squandered their pension funds and retired military husbands' savings.

You better take a step back and thoroughly think things through – 'ponder the path of your feet' (Proverbs 4:26) before seeking to hastily get rich and taking a huge misstep that turns your life upside down in an instant.

Ponder the paths of the people you associate, run with and have "fun" with lest their unethical and illegal behavior trip you up. Show me your friends and I will show you your future. Guilt by association happens rather easily when the law shows up and you have little time to make excuses or give explanations. TV cameras and networks edit "the news" and statements made to distort the totality of things said to create controversy and sensationalism, by which the media keeps viewers glued and tuned in.

Beware lest you become the next "story" and your sudden fall become media fodder and the next scandal. 'Guard your heart, which is the wellspring of life' (Proverbs 4:23).

Beware of seductive, godless and impure women – some being gold diggers, others just looking for another free party and thrill. 'Ponder the path of life, knowing her ways are moveable, that you cannot know them' (Proverbs 5:6).

Get back to your house before the sun goes down at night and try to be in before midnight to prevent the demons roaming the streets in the dark night hours from accessing and harming your life.

No matter how outwardly beautiful a woman is, if her speech is impure and her ways slippery; run from her, because she is a disaster waiting to happen. If a woman cannot shut her mouth and listen to people speaking… If she alone has to be the center of attention… If she is more concerned with her makeup and outward look than her inner character, pack your bags and run from her brother! If a woman cannot keep a job, but only lives off her looks; RUN FROM HER! She has nothing to give you but aggravation, heartache and pain.

Any momentary sexual pleasure is not worth a lifetime of pain when she gets pregnant and wants you to parent her children. Beware of gold diggers! Some women have no education, no skills, no humility, and no desire to change or further develop themselves. If all they want to do is stay at home and watch Jerry Springer and Kim Kardashian while you go to work, do yourself a favor (if you're not married to them already) and RUN!

Ladies, know assuredly the reverse is true, as this message is not about gender but about integrity of heart and the issues of life. So if your man (or the man pursuing you) doesn't have a solid job, has no vision for his life, isn't going anywhere, and only wants to sweet talk you to get in your pants; pack your bags and run from him!

I'm writing and talking as I would to my own brother and sister (and future children). Don't waste your time and precious life telling yourself lies. You're not going to change anybody! Don't flatter yourself by believing otherwise. Only God can change people and most people won't even listen to God.

Most people just call upon God to meet their needs, not to change their character and ways. God however is not Santa Claus to be called on to merely bestow gifts to you.

Before asking God to open His hand, you better take a look into His eyes and awaken to God's heart and mind regarding His will for your life and any areas of reformation needed in your character and conduct.

God has already given every human being gifts, talents and abilities; but few fully attend to them thoroughly to develop and use them to the maximum of their capability. This is a sad travesty, a person to whom God has given gifts, talents and abilities and yet they cannot see the treasures hidden and deposited deep within them.

It's your responsibility to develop yourself and that which God has given you. God will not carry you to the Promised Land. You have to walk there one foot in front of the other.

Some pray for miracles. God will do miracles sometimes, but not all the time. We must live by faith (Romans 1:17) and work with God (Mark 16:20). God won't let you lay on your butt eating chocolates and do everything for you. You must get up, hear from heaven, develop your gifts, get busy and go forward with vision!

No as for those lazy, lackadaisical lawn guys who did a halfhearted job only looking for a paycheck, do you think I will ever use them again? Of course not!

Do you think I will ever invite the yelling, disrespectful, double charging washing machine repairman back into my home! Hell no!

Do you think God is going to bless us when we are lazy and unwilling to read His Word, pray, work hard and use our gifts for His glory? Of course not!

Beware of big talkers. People who are really going somewhere in life don't have time for long, prolonged, lengthy conversations about trivial things that care no weight, bearing or significance. They have a vision and are going somewhere. They don't need to waste their breath trying to sell you on their greatness. They are busy doing what they know to do. Big mouths and cheap talk are distractions to them.

People who just want to hear themselves talk and monopolize conversations to gratify their egos and insecurities are useless to your life. Save your time and guard it well. Manage your time more strictly and protectively than your money, because you can always get more money, but time goes and never returns.

Our life consists of time, moments, seconds, hours, days, months, years and ultimately these all add up to a lifetime. Time is blazing by daily and unless we guard our focus and attend to our to do list with an arrow like fierce focus, we will be easily distracted with social media, arguing about stupid stuff we cannot change, and wasting our lives.

So count the cost in every friendship, relationship, interaction, business dealing, and future endeavor. Ask yourself, what is the worst thing that can come from this? What is the best thing? Thoroughly think it through and wholeheartedly examine the consequences of your actions and decisions BEFOREHAND. If you will do so, be prudent in all of your ways, you will save yourself much heartache and pain.

Also ask yourself WHY do I really want this? WHY do I so much want to be with this person? Is it motivated by your personal insecurity, ego, ambition, greed, lust, or fear? Get down deep inside and ask yourself the tough questions.

As you do, you will better be able to navigate your life and guard against distractions. Likewise you will become more self-aware, whereby you can not only be brutally honest with yourself, but equally be more respectful and honoring toward others feelings, time and pursuits.

People are not put in this world just to gratify your lusts, be used for your ambition, be milked for money, or serve as pawns on your chessboard. Love, respect and honor people!

If you fail to do so, life will surely send innumerable circumstances to grind down your motives, humble you and get your attention.

When a thief broke into a California home and heard "Jesus is watching you." He didn't see anybody, but heard a voice. Again all of the sudden, he heard: "Jesus is watching you!" The thief then noticed a parrot. "What is your name?" asked the thief. "Clarence" replied the parrot.

The thief standing arrogantly in the home in which he had just broken into remarked: "Ha ha! Who names a parrot Clarence?"

The parrot replied, "The same people who named that pit bull over there Jesus."

Remember don't just think of yourself when going about your daily routine. Always be mindful that Jesus is watching you!

6. TRUTH

Tell the truth, keep your word and don't cut corners.

West Point lives by the motto: "Don't lie, cheat, steal, or tolerate those who do." Associating with losers and people uncommitted to a life of integrity is a sure way to screw up your life and rob your destiny. Because eventually when they get in trouble, you may soon find yourself in prison with them by reason of guilt by association.

Pastor Joel Osteen shares a story about how a generous business man who gave a struggling home builder an opportunity to build him a home. The shrewd home builder cut many corners to increase his profit margin and winded up building a poor quality home as a result. Upon completion of the home, the business man held out the keys to the home to the builder saying, "Here. I want to bless you with this home. I've already got a home of my own. I just wanted to be a blessing to you."

It's worth remembering, how we work for and treat the property of others determines whether or not God can entrust us with our own. Honor the property of others and their hard work. Life isn't always about you, or what you possess. When you can humbly honor others and their accomplishments, God in turn will favor and eventually honor you. You reap what you sow. Give of yourself to extend and bestow honor to those so deserving. Eventually it will boomerang back to you as you do!

I'm appalled to see the way the guys at the local *LA Fitness* where I exercise treat our gym. They use paper towels, but after using them instead of discarding them in the waste basket, throw them on the floor for the janitor to pick up.

Water bottles are strewn across the workout floor, not discarded in the trash can where they go. People use gym equipment and leave a puddle of sweat behind when they are done, not wiping up after themselves. Unlike years ago when I began working out at the gym with my father, few in my "health" club use towels to keep the equipment clean and free from their sweat and stench.

This doesn't make for a very pleasant place to work out. Nevertheless the equipment is quite new and nice (better than most I use in the 70 countries I have traveled to overseas), but the people, the gym members, many lack class, self-respect and common courtesy enough to clean up after themselves.

Unfortunately, this entitlement mentality is growing across our country and causing our nation to fall in stature globally, economically, academically and in a multiplicity of areas. Unless our President and leaders address the matter of integrity and character (an intangible that doesn't always appear on a financial balance sheet, but most certainly impacts the bottom line), our nation is going to fall even further and greatly.

You see the intangible of integrity is something the human eye doesn't see so readily or easily, it is a matter of the heart – something only the person and God the Creator notice. But know surely if gone unaddressed and unharnessed, individuals, marriages, families, companies, communities and countries will feel the effects of lack of integrity.

Therefore be faithful to your employer and that which God has entrusted you with (your time, talents, relationships, resources and opportunities)

To whom much is given, much is required (Luke 12:48).

When you are a foursquare, solid, straight shooter and trust worthy person – God and people will value and trust you with opportunities and more than you can imagine.

When you tell the truth, you tell people they can trust you. When you hold to the truth, even to your own heart and don't sell out for momentary gratification and gain, you send a signal to the world that you are different and a grade above the rest.

Who shall abide and remain in God's holy tabernacle? Who shall ascend to and dwell on God's holy hill? 'He that walks uprightly, and works righteousness, and speaks the truth in his heart. He that does not backbite with his tongue, nor do evil to his neighbor, nor take up a reproach against his neighbor. In whose eyes a vile person is contemned; but he honors them that fear the LORD. He that swears to his own hurt, and changes not. He that does not put out his money to usury, nor takes reward against the innocent. He that does these things shall never be moved' (Psalm 15:1-5).

When you make a commitment and agree to something, do you 'swear to your own hurt'? In other words, do you hold to your word even when it becomes inconvenient and uncomfortable? Do you hold to your own agreements and adhere to your own signed contracts, or do you manipulate and maneuver to change the terms in your favor?

These are things that determine the depth and strength of our character (or the lack thereof). These are the little details that can become devilish tendencies and subtleties by which our character is tainted and reputation muddied by reason of poor quality decisions.

Character is made by making good decisions regardless of the repercussions, circumstances and consequences. I recall once when my bank account was getting low last year. Meanwhile I had contracted with some employees to do a couple jobs for me. When the money got low, I could have asked them to wait and paid them later. Instead I paid them and suffered through having just 4 cents in my bank account for two weeks, while my wife was away on vacation visiting friends and family in Canada.

I didn't eat so well those two weeks, living off old grains in my Tupperware, water and not much more; but it felt good to pay my employees, finalize the terms of my agreement on those contracts and complete those assignments. It wasn't long before God again provided and took care of my needs and enabled me to get back to living large and in charge with food in my refrigerator.

Make the hard decisions and God will come through for you and show Himself strong repeatedly time and time again.

Tell the truth! Don't cut corners. When things change, communicate what is going on to your creditors and employees, but don't expect them to alter the affairs of their lives for you.

Creditors actually will usually give you some grace, payment extensions, and waive late payment penalties if you are forthright and call them in advance to let them know what is going on with you financially. Being proactive works in your favor even when you are struggling financially.

I know because I've been there after I was hit by a drunk driver, my car totaled, my body injured and my bills mounting up. Nevertheless God proved Himself to be faithful, giving me peace through every storm.

Having studied debt arbitration and serving as a debt arbitrator and consultant, I understand turbulent and trying economic times. Your creditors do as well. Heck, many states in the U.S. and county municipal governments are also bankrupt. Walt Disney declared bankruptcy 3 times and Donald Trump at least once himself.

Just because you struggle for a season financially doesn't mean you are unsuccessful. Successful people take great chances sometimes to make sizeable gains and advances. When it doesn't work out, you do your best to carry on and figure it out as you go forward not living and looking in the rearview mirror (since you cannot change the past any way …although you certainly can learn from it).

As a company owner and manager, if you're going to be the big boss and lead with excellence and integrity, you have to be willing to work without pay before you ask that of your employees. Pay your employees first, lest they get angry and attack you (and what you together have built).

My father used to build houses for 20 years. In the home building industry contractors get what is called "draws" from banks after each stage of a home is constructed. In other words banks are not going to give unscrupulous contractors a lump sum of cash to leave the country and go on vacation in the Caribbean, while telling them they are "building" a house.

My dad was an honest home builder, but like everyone else he had to play by the rules and wait for the bank to release his funds after every stage of construction. Sometimes this meant awaiting an inspector to come to a job site to inspect and approve completed tasks of the construction process before the next "draw" was released.

I recall as a 12 year-old boy a foul mouth block mason getting angry at my father for not paying him on a Friday. He appeared to have big plans to go out and party that weekend and didn't understand the delays of inspections for work completed. His foreman however did, but the laborer would not be persuaded.

This 225 pound block mason towered at about 6'2 and had a hot temper. Yet to my surprise, my dad (in his mid-to-late 30s at the time) had a temper to match and it wasn't long before my dad had heard enough of this hot mouthed man. Dad jumped out of his truck, tackled the block mason, got him in a headlock and wouldn't let go.

I was a bit concerned that had my dad let go, this block mason might have thrown some heavy blows. The foreman, a middle aged man, had a level head and more tender heart. Thankfully he and his other block masons didn't all attack my dad, but just let the loud mouth block mason and my dad go at it.

While the loud mouth was in a head lock, my 5'11" dad was eventually coaxed out of the scrapple by the foreman and thankfully no further blows were thrown. Needless to say after that altercation the loud mouth mason stopped talking and few words were said thereafter.

Of course the masons were paid, but not the very day big mouth wanted. So the lesson to be learned here is sometimes it is advantageous for us to be slow to speak and quick to hear. Everybody is dealing with different struggles, scenarios and troubles in life.

Life is not always so easy as when we were 6 years old and just turned on the morning cartoons and had a bowl of cereal in front of the TV.

Harnessing our mouths, managing our emotions, acting with wisdom and behaving with integrity requires great restraint and discipline. This is why surrounding yourself with people like minded with a similar commitment to live with integrity is so important. Otherwise people pursuing immediate gratification (a me, myself and I approach to life) will easily jade and taint you.

Hence the wisdom of West Point's motto: "Don't lie, cheat, steal, or tolerate those who do."

You see, what you tolerate will perpetuate and eventually grow to soon dominate. You therefore must keep your eyes and ears open to address subtle incorrect attitudes and mindsets in yourself, your family and organization. Otherwise these little wrong attitudes (often heard and conveyed through communication and conversation) will fester and grow, spreading their toxicity, bitterness and deadly poison to infect your family and organization.

Making hard decisions and doing what is right isn't easy, but it always feels good and enables you to sleep well with peace at the end of the day.

When I go to Whole Foods and buy organic figs, I could just as easily mark the bag with another number for conventional figs (which usually sell for a dollar less). But this is an opportunity for me to cultivate my character and integrity, build and further fortify my heart and mind upon a foundation of what is pure and right.

Build and construct a fortress of purity and integrity within yourself and God will honor you in due time and bless you beyond your wildest dreams. Your truthful and honest living will not go unnoticed.

Be true and pure, because God will thereby favor and bless you!

7. HONOR

Remember a good name is better than riches (see Proverbs 22:1).

Self-worth and wealth begins within.   The strongest and fastest horses are useless unless they can be harnessed.

Everybody influences somebody. Even when you are not looking, someone surely is watching you. Be your best and as you do, someone surely will be blessed. And at the end of your life, someone will show up to speak nicely and well of you. Plus with a bit of favor from God, people who see your good character will want to befriend you and give you opportunities.

Your name and reputation carries more weight and worth in the marketplace than how much money you have in your bank. Value your name, integrity, reputation and self-worth over financials and you will attract wealth and opportunities BECAUSE OF WHO YOU ARE.

When WHO YOU ARE is right, what you HAVE will take care of itself. More important, what you DO and HAVE is NOT WHO YOU ARE! Never forget that!

I'm reminded of a scene in the first Wall Street movie near the end when Charlie Sheen's father rebukes him for being all about the almighty dollar and selling his soul and dignity to pursue profit. Charlie's dad meanwhile worked for an airline and labor union faithfully all his life, but slept peacefully at night and maintained his self-respect not getting connected to shady and unsavory characters like Gordon Gecko.

Billionaire Bernie Madoff made a ton of money on ponzie schemes on Wall Street, but lost his dignity, and will die in prison for defrauding countless people who believed in him. Madoff's own son committed suicide after enduring the shame of being associated with his father, I bet Bernie Madoff would give all of his money if he could have his son back and alive again.

What good is it to gain the whole world and have all the possessions at your fingertips, if in so doing therewith you must sell and forfeit your own soul and personal dignity? What can you give in exchange for your soul? (see Mark 8:36-38)

Remember our life is not found in the abundance of the things that we possess (Luke 12:15). Who cares if our neighbors and friends get caught up in the frenzy of possessions, competing and comparing! We don't have to succumb to such an infantile mentality, which is life diminishing and deadly.

When you allow yourself to be put on a treadmill of performance and live only for stuff (or the way you look in the eyes of others), you sell yourself short and short-circuit your true calling. It becomes difficult to hear your own inner voice when you are so mesmerized and locked into the opinions and thoughts of others about you. If this spirit of fear drives you to live up to others whims, wants and expectations for your life; break free from this and live FREE today!

Be mindful of the people who love, respect and look to you to be a role model and example. Love those who look to you for light, life, inspiration and guidance enough to behave and act with a heart of excellence.

When you predetermine to be your best and live at a level of peak performance, you position yourself to daily step into greatness and attract blessings your way.

8. HUMILITY

Humility allows you to take responsibility for wrongdoing and come out on top for doing so. My father sometimes could be hot tempered when I was a child. Yet to my surprise, sometimes dad would come back to me and apologize. I greatly respected my father for being self-aware and humble enough to admit his own wrongdoing.

As Pastor Benny Hinn taught me in Bible School training, "Never trust a man who cannot use his eraser." In other words if a man cannot own his mistakes and be willing to course correct, you cannot trust, work, or go very far with him.

Life is a learning process. Maya Angelou has said, "If I had known better, I would have done better." We too must remember we are learning and growing along our life journey. Once it seems like we have mastered adulthood, then suddenly we become a spouse. Then once we finely feel secure about being a husband, or wife; then we are parents. The demands of life often can just keep growing and getting heavier upon us.

We therefore must be patient with ourselves and others. Thankfully I entered these various stages of manhood, marriage and fatherhood slowly with many years in between. Others are not so fortunate and enter them all simultaneously.

As we are compassionate with ourselves and others, we open the door for humility of heart and God's grace to help us. Don't be so hard on yourself or others. It makes life far too difficult, demanding and burdensome.

Keep a sense of humor and humility, not taking yourself too seriously. Take life and its many challenges seriously, but be willing to laugh at yourself along the way as you grow, mature and strive to master the many demands and nuances life.

As a child I recall my dad and stepmom fighting and bickering for a good 10 years early in their marriage, but somehow they always managed to look back in retrospect and have a good laugh when reflecting on their behavior and trying situations.

Today mom and dad have been married 35 years and are going strong. I believe a sense of humor and their ability be lighthearted through all the challenges of life has probably been the number one secret to their marital success.

Although I was voted the funniest in my high school class, I can be a bit intense and must remind myself to laugh through life. This makes everything easier and opens the door for spontaneous creative problem solving. It's hard to be creative when you are uptight, but when you learn how to play with pain and perform under pressure with a smile on your face the flow of creative ideas to master your problems becomes more readily available.

In the movie *It's a Beautiful Life* a father and his son are in a concentration camp in Germany. It's a very challenging situation, which could break down the spirit of most people. But this special father told his son it was a game. When the German soldiers appeared barking orders, the father would translate what was said to his son in game terminology to make the ordeal more fun and seem less life threatening.

Eventually when the war was over, the small boy emerged from imprisonment walking freely down a street surrounded by U.S. ally Army tanks and was unharmed. The boy actually got picked up and put in one of those tanks to look down from up high and see what it was like to ride in a big tank.

The film shows us that no matter how grueling and challenging the circumstances in which we find ourselves are, we can choose how we frame them in the movie screens of our mind and explain them verbally in terminology that are less dramatic and more bearable so we are not overcome by fear of the unknown and things beyond our control. Often the way we frame and see things internally is everything and ultimately determines how we approach a predicament or problem.

Remain light hearted, playful, and keep a sense of humor. Be humble and quick to admit your errors, taking responsibility for your actions, missteps and miscalculations. As you do, you will win the trust of your family, peers, friends, employees and competitors. Buying the truth over being concerned with self-exaltation always wins the trust of others in the long run.

Humility recognizes others accomplishments, contributions and insight of others; while also acknowledging you are not perfect and make mistakes. Such a mindset endears people to you and makes your family and organization stronger.

When you error, make a mistake, mess up, or offend someone APOLOGIZE for it and MAKE IT RIGHT to the best of your ability.

Never trust a person who cannot use their eraser, apologize for wrongdoing, admit to any fault, or acknowledge any weakness in their character.

It's better to be honest and transparent, rather than oversell sell yourself, under deliver and have to live with knowing you disappointed people.

9. FORGIVE

Be forgiving and give people a chance to change, grow, mature and be transformed. Don't let offenses contaminate your soul, make you bitter, weigh you down emotionally and thwart your focus mentally.

Life can be challenging enough as it is when your soul is not encumbered with relational problems and unresolved issues. When however you allow unforgiveness to burden your soul, life becomes much more heavy and hard as you become further entangled emotionally.

Thankfully God is love (1John 4:16) and is patient with us. Patience is the first adjective God uses to describe the word love (see 1Corinthians 13:4).

When we are impatient with others we proudly elevate ourselves to the place of God, which sets us up to be judged and disciplined by God for being judgmental. Jesus warned that when we refuse to forgive, God in heaven will deliver us over to the tormentors (see Matthew 18:33-35). I believe the torment is both on earth as we wrestle with the emotional sorrows and agony of unforgiveness and when we reach eternity, where we must give an account to God for our unwillingness to forgive others as our loving heavenly Father has forgiven us.

Blessed are the merciful, because they too shall obtain mercy (Matthew 5:7).

We all make mistakes and have no idea what anybody else has fully been through on their life journey. Therefore leave judgment to God. Believe the best about people until they prove you wrong and then pray for them to grow in grace and mature.

When you believe the best about people, they do more to live up to your expectations and please you. Unconditional love isn't abundant in supply in the earth, nor easily found everywhere. Gossip, slander, backbiting and ridiculing tongues are plenteous and quick to demean human beings. Such a way of life is demonic and deadly relationally and professionally.

As Pastor Paula White once said, "If someone will gossip to you, they will gossip about you." I believe this to be true and a way by which to evaluate the character of those with whom you interact relationally, socially and professionally.

When unconditional love is found in you, people will honor and value you, knowing that you see the good in them when nobody else does. Believe the best about people realizing that we all have room for improvement and that God is not done with any of us.

God can save to the uttermost and reach down and touch and transform a mass murderer in prison. God can supernaturally melt the hardest of hearts. God knows how to intervene and orchestrate circumstances in a person's life so as to bring people across their path who are just as vile and undone as they are; to serve as a mirror to show them areas in their own life that must change and be transformed.

When we relinquish control, let go of pride, and let God do His job without us trying to get in the way and play the judge; then Almighty God will have His way and get people's attention.

I recall being on a cruise ship with my parents on their 30th year wedding anniversary, when my brother was drinking and acting up. My younger brother was drunk every night on the ship, waking me up after midnight to pick a fight. Not wanting to cause my parents any trouble and pain, I had to grin and bear this 6 foot monster in my cabin (a small cabin with no window or balcony).

Looking forward to the ports of call and getting off the ship to enjoy the various islands, I didn't want to be distracted by my drunk brother. I wanted to sleep. So as to not further enflame his anger, I just slept on the floor of my parents' cabin.

When I had reached my breaking point one night with my brother, I prayed: "Lord, you say in your Word that it is a righteous thing with God to recompense tribulation to them that trouble us (2Thessalonians 1:6). Please fight against my brother on my behalf so I don't have to and break him down so I can have some peace."

I know God fights for His kids (see Exodus 14:25) and defends His people (Psalm 18:6-20).

The word 'recompense' means – to give compensation to; pay for; return in kind; reimburse. God will not remain silent, but will surely speak somehow be it through circumstances, struggles, law enforcement and others who will push back upon the ungodly in the earth and stop them in their tracks.

That night when my brother left the cabin to hit the bars and get drunk, I slept in peace. The next morning when I woke up, the brother who had been terrorizing me had blood down his shirt. When I asked what happened to him, he said he fell down. LOL

God knows how to knock a person down from their lofty high horse and high-mindedness. Surely 'the righteous shall be recompensed in the earth: much more the wicked and the sinner' (Proverbs 11:31).

As for the righteous, God promises in His Word to reward them who diligently seek Him (Hebrews 11:6) and endeavor to do that which is right in His sight.

Be at peace no matter what circumstance in which you find yourself. Forgive and give grace to people yes, but don't allow people to use and abuse you. Value yourself and guard your precious life, time, focus, and purpose as well. Never respect or go out of your way for a person who doesn't respect and honor you. If you do so, consider it an act of compassion and mercy. But as for people who prey on you and use you repeatedly for their own self-willed agenda, there comes a time to say no and let them grow up and stop using you.

We all fall once in a while, but be willing to get back up, learn from the past, try again and go forward. The righteous may fall, but they always get back up (see Proverbs 24:16), overcome and succeed!

10. DISCERNMENT

Be discerning and make wise decisions considering the consequences of your actions beforehand.

Gut wrenching stories such as the Florida dermatologist Dr. Michael Rosin who lied to the elderly telling them they had skin cancer and cutting up their faces to make $2,000 a cut when the surgeries were unnecessary burns me up inside.

One elderly Pastor was cut 70 times, all later found to be unnecessary surgeries. Yes, the fraudulent and immoral dermatologist eventually was thrown in jail and exposed, but the poor elderly man who spent years of his life in fear, thinking he had cancer, and now has a mutilated face cannot reclaim what he lost.

http://www.cnbc.com/id/28777032

Thus it is vital that we exercise discernment, do our homework on people and ensure we are dealing with reputable people before haphazardly entrusting them with our health and wellbeing.

I was bruised by a dermatologist in Soho, Manhattan, New York City who claimed this procedure would likely remove the red spots on the side of my face. The dermatologist however withheld some vital information I would have liked to have known beforehand.

Blindly believing what I was told by the attractive young dermatologist, I let her perform the procedure. To her credit, the dermatologist did forewarn me I would be bruised for 2 weeks before my face would heal, after which the red spots would likely go away.

Upon beginning to zap me with some device that sounded like firecrackers, my face was immediately burned and I collapsed passing out. Upon falling to the floor and forgetting where I was, I heard the Filipino nurse and Indian doctor talking to me asking me if I was alright. Not knowing where I was, nor what had just happened, it took me a while to regroup.

The two ladies put me on a chair to lay down and brought me some water. Then the dermatologist left the room and later returned with a legal document (a liability release form) she asked me to sign. Upon reading the legal release of liability for the procedure, it mentioned the procedure potentially could cause harm to my eyes and have other ugly side effects.

Angry, I had not been told all of this before the procedure, I did not sign the legal document. More concerned about my black and blue face, I wanted to cry the minute I saw myself in the mirror. I lived with this horrific appearance for 3 weeks (longer than I was told at 2 weeks).

What bothered me the most was the excruciating discomfort socially as I couldn't really do anything without people wandering what had happened to me? Understandably, as I looked like a leper – a contagious disease few probably would want to be near.

When after three weeks of applying arnica gel the black and blue marks finally went away, but the red marks on my face remained. Thus I had just wasted 3 weeks of my life and paid $250 to do so. When I asked the dermatologist for a refund, she refused me.

This is the problem with modern day medicine, a huge racket and industry. Most doctors deal with and treat symptoms, never dealing with, or attending to the underlying problem internally. After buying thousands of dollars of books on health, cancer, biology, detoxification, and other topics I discovered by cleaning my liver and changing my diet I could heal and improve the condition of my skin.

As a former fitness trainer I now serve as a health coach to a handful of clients every year to help them improve their health and achieve wellness body-mind-spirit. So from this gruesome ordeal, I was able to save myself and now help others.

Yet if I could have done the whole thing over again and were able to relive that season of my life; I would have just read the books first, taken my health into my own hands, and if ever I felt unsure, I would have seen a naturopath or acupuncturist first before entrusting my wellbeing into a medical doctor (the latter trained at medical schools financed by pharmaceutical companies).

Discernment undoubtedly will make or break you in many areas of your life. Health and wellness body-mind-spirit is the most important to attend to before all others.

Life consists of time, which is precious. Guard your focus and eliminate distractions.

Do so graciously and wisely so as to not offend people, but if they are offended, don't worry about it. People who get offended, that is their problem not yours.

Put the answer machine on. Instruct a secretary to take your calls. Only reply to calls and emails you truly value and deem important to your personal progress, purpose and life mission. Delete and don't listen to the rest unless you are feeling compassionate and merciful.

Remember the phone is there for your use, not for you to be mastered and used by it. Turn off the phone often to attend to your work and return phone calls rather than feeling obligated to answer the phone the instant it rings.

When someone knocks at your door, look through the peep hole and if you don't see anybody on the other side you care to talk to; then go back to work and ignore the distraction.

My mom was a drug addict and alcoholic who died before my grandparents because she liked to date the bad boys and wouldn't honor, respect and listen to her parents. She was killed by an 18 year-old drunk driver, she being only 49 years of age when she died.

I could have felt forever sorry for my mom and allowed her to monopolize my life (as she did much of my grandparents' days and nights). Yet I knew by watching years of their interactions that my mom had nothing to add, but only came to subtract and get what she wanted.

I therefore had no time or tolerance for her self-absorbed and self-willed behavior. I noticed she would raise her voice and yell when she didn't get what she wanted. I recall her pushing my grandma to the ground and breaking her arm once and years later breaking Nana's leg (always because my "mother" wasn't given what she wanted and was angry).

One year my mom tried to do a karate kick on my grandfather right between the legs. Eventually my grandparents wised up and put a restraining order on the devilish woman to keep her out of their home.

When I came back from two years of living and ministering throughout Asia, I stayed with my grandparents to care for them in their old age (as they had taken care of me serving as my parents in my younger years). One early morning around 2am as I recall my mother showed up ringing the doorbell like a mad woman trying to get into the house. When I saw through the window it was her, I calmly picked up the telephone and called the police. When the police arrived, she was escorted off the premises.

I know that doesn't seem very compassionate and perhaps like a contradiction to some of the other things I have written, but there is no formula or standard we must apply continually in every situation. On the contrary, each situation will bring with it unique people and peculiar circumstances. You must feel your way through each one and discern the temperament, demeanor and details of each situation and then make a decision how to act rather than respond out of emotion or a sense of obligation.

I had little obligation to my "mother" since she was never there for me and only caused my grandparents and me trouble. Beyond giving birth to me (and I'm sure she was smoking when I was in the womb because I was born with pneumonia), my mom did little for me as a child and adult.

Therefore when she showed up on fire from hell to wake us all up and demand her wants, I said no thanks and phoned the police to get rid of her. There is a time and place for everything. She could have come during the day when we were all awake (as would any normal person), but again "mom" was all about herself and disregarded the feelings of others.

Even if she had been in a troublesome situation and needed help, she could have rang the doorbell once or twice and patiently waited rather than ringing the doorbell nonstop like a mad woman. These subtle nuances and details reveal a person's demeanor, spirit, heart and mind. Don't override what these details and nonverbal cues are telling you.

I wouldn't have allowed anyone else outside of my family to come to my home and wake me up at 2am in such a way. Therefore family or not, I called the police to get rid of such a disturbance and hopefully teach the woman a lesson how to conduct herself around me.

When my brother showed up several years later (long after my grandparents had passed) on a Monday morning drunk wanting to come into my home and "hang out," I also refused him. Why? Because I work during the day and don't have time for drunks!

If you want to spend time with me, you better be prepared to do it sober; because I have no desire to hang out with drunks and derelicts who just want to waste my time. I value and want to invest, not squander my time.

You see what you tolerate will perpetuate and continue to show up and circulate in your life. What you tolerate will grow and come to dominate unless you say no and demand otherwise.

My goofy "mother" may have driven my grandparents nuts, but she wasn't going to torment me! I knew how to deal with her and her devils. And no I didn't feel sorry for her, because her life was directed by her own choices and stubbornness when she disregarded the wise counsel of her parents.

Obey and honor your parents and your life will be well and long on the earth (Exodus 20:12; Ephesians 6:2-3). Disobey and dishonor your parents and your life will be cut short. In other words, God Himself doesn't really want to keep some people around for too long on the earth because they are more of a curse and nuisance to others than a blessing.

That is precisely how I felt about my "mother" who honestly I was relieved when I heard the news that she died. In actuality I was somewhat sad for her (as I know she didn't fulfill her potential and purpose), but at the same time relieved and pleased for my grandparents because the madness could finally be stopped so they could have some peaceful years without their devil of a daughter.

It was bitter sweet, but nevertheless tragic that such a talented woman (a cheerleader, honor student in high school, university graduate) could be so duped by bad boys who just wanted to get in her bed.

My mom's generation was hardcore drug users, experimenting with stuff nobody should be putting in their bodies. It is no wonder so many drugs are now legalized and being pushed on children from birth. The druggies of the 1960's are now medical doctors and pharmacists legalizing much of the stuff, today preying on a new generation. These mind-altering drugs sadly are even being pushed on small children by the pharmaceutical industry and TV commercials.

We all have God given gifts, which must be guarded and guided. My mother was greatly gifted, intelligent and beautiful. But she failed to guard her gifts and opened herself up to the wrong kind of people. The "party" lifestyle and crowd never added to her. It only diminished and distracted my momr, while dislocating her from her purpose to be a lawyer.

Discernment is something parents often fail to teach their children. Thus as kids enter their teenage years they often are duped by their "friends" who my grandfather told me if you removed the letter 'r' from friends what do you get? Fiends!

The devil doesn't use strangers to destroy your life. Hell uses people in close proximity to get at and destroy you. Be discerning and make wise decisions so your life can be long, well, enjoyable and meaningful.

Protect yourself realizing that some decisions last and stay with you for a lifetime. The young men doing drugs with my mom were able to leave the dope behind and move on with their lives. Not my mom, as she became ensnared.

You never know what may ensnare your soul and forever drain the life of God out of you. Therefore beware and make wise decisions knowing sometimes life is like walking through a minefield in which there are some deadly weapons which can forever alter, maim, lame, wound and wreck your life.

Show me your friends and I will show you your future. Who you hang with determines how far and where you will go in life. Had my mother chosen friends who did not drink alcohol, refused drugs and lived sober meaningful lives; she would not have found herself in so many compromising and life altering predicaments.

Living with integrity is like eating healthy – it takes discernment, discipline, commitment and a willingness to take the time to ask some hard questions. Conventional or organic? Farm raised or wild? Any food additives, preservatives, or chemical colorings I should be aware of? Genetically modified?

It's amazing at restaurants how few patrons ask these questions and just eat whatever is put in front of them. Certainly this makes it easy for restaurant owners to enlarge their profit margins, while feeding customers less than healthy "food."

Life is no different. Few ask the hard questions and dare to get beneath the surface in conversations, to figure out what drives people. Motivations are often communicated in conversation, but many times we are not actively listening to the words being said.

The art of communication is listening, not talking. We all can talk, but it takes discernment and a keen intuition to actively listen. It takes wisdom and skill to know how to ask the right questions to discern if a person is the ideal life partner for you, or if you should do business with someone.

Asking critical questions will save you a lifetime of pain and heartache if you will take the time to do so. Companies read each other's balance sheets and do a thorough evaluation before ever making an acquisition or performing a merger to combine their strengths.

Shouldn't relationships be equally as smart and purposeful before we commit to one another for a lifetime? Hormones and chemistry are all good and well – certainly enjoyable for a time, but once you merge love and life together, what will you get and find? Many no longer want what they've got, once they get what they once wanted.

These hard questions beforehand will give you a glimpse into the future and save you from embarking on the sea of matrimony followed by a rough turbulent ride.

There are many tempting parking places on the road to success. Consistently pray for God to sharpen your discernment, strengthen your spirit, and enable you to overcome temptation. Listen to your instincts and gut within. Ask the Holy Spirit, the spirit of wisdom and revelation (Ephesians 1:17-19), to show you things about people and situations.

If it doesn't feel right, don't get involved until you feel peace within. Let the peace of God rule your heart, mind and direct your life (see Philippians 4:6-7). Say no without feeling guilty. Live authentically without apology.

Beyond behavior, listen to and examine people's words. From the overflow of the heart come the words of the mouth (Luke 6:45). Some people have treasures of wisdom and life experiences hidden within their hearts, whereas others have toxicity, unforgiveness and stinking thinking eating them up and festering within.

Take some time to talk to people before committing to go with them on a longer journey of life, or partnering in a project. As you do, you will better be able to gauge if this is a person you want to go somewhere with or run from. Often a simple phone call and a few minutes listening to what is in them will tell you all you need to know.

To test what a person says, ask yourself – "Would you teach this to children?"

Adults somehow make allowances for improper motivations, pursuits and ill-conceived outlooks on the world. We get jaded along the way of life and in the business world can begin to put profit before people; or pleasure over principle. Yet this will never serve us well in the long run, neither in the many other areas of our life.

Because once a mindset gets embedded and rooted within us, it will begin to grow, permeate and circulate in other dealings and conversations with people. Therefore sometimes we need to conduct a personal inventory of our values, thoughts, beliefs and disposition to ensure we are properly positioned for love, life and success.

Otherwise despite all our hard work and efforts, we will repel the very opportunities and people we most desire and need in our lives. The foundation within must be pure before we can attract a promotion and go to the next level in our lives. Not all promotions are attainable by our own hard work and diligent efforts.

If you are already a CEO and run your own company, it may seem like you have already arrived and have no need to further ascend upward in life. Not so! There is always room for personal growth in some area of our lives.

Maybe it is relationally, socially, or physically. Perhaps we need to better cultivate peace within and life balance for inner harmony. These are many things I work with executives on when serving as a life coach.

The outward appearance projects that all is well in the business world, but the truth is successful CEOs and directors of companies also have problems and struggles. Marriage is tough stuff no matter who you are. That is because we cannot control or lord ourselves over people.

Getting along and happily living and working with people is an art. It is like a dance and every dance partner is different. It requires intuition, spontaneity, social grace and sincerity.

Beware of limiting beliefs that demonize others, diminish the human spirit and dwarf your potential. Loving and allowing people to freely be themselves also requires great discipline of leaders who know how to influence and shape people. Yet we have to be careful during the shaping process to not manipulate, control and try to conform people to our image; lest we remove who they are altogether and they become deeply bitter towards us.

Every person is entitled to a professional and personal life. Knowing our boundaries as leaders is vital so we can love, nurture, nourish and respect people allowing them to live authentic fulfilling lives.

Invest in and help develop your people, while giving them the freedom to explore their gifts, talents, abilities and deeper lifelong calling. If that means one day they leave your company and you, so be it. Prize their happiness and cherish their personal fulfillment.

Often times criticism is nothing more than a cover up for a person's own insecurities, unfinished business and unresolved issues. Before you criticize your employees and the people in your life, be quick to acknowledge their strengths and praise them for that which they excel in. Also be thankful and show gratitude for the blessing each person is in your life. Even those who sometimes seem to be less than a blessing (like my mother), know they are often there in your life only for a time and that they too teach us something about life, people and ourselves.

Life can be a struggle at times, but it doesn't always have to be a battle. Be patient. Be kind. Be discerning. Trust your abilities and know you can navigate through the nuances of life peacefully and skillfully no matter what comes your way.

Listen more than you speak. Be a lifelong learner committed to personal growth. Use the two ears on the side of your head more often and frequently.

By doing so you will learn more, connect better with people, grow in knowledge, wisdom and understanding and be a person others like to be around.

Cultivating integrity gives you inner strength, feels good, breeds confidence and enables you to stand with composure through trials and tribulations, and overcome the challenges and storms of life when others are being tossed to and fro.

None of us are perfect, but let's strive to have humble hearts and live with integrity to the best of our ability.

11. BE THANKFUL

When you are grateful, you can truly and daily step into greatness. Cultivating an attitude of gratitude tells God you are thankful for the gift of life and the many blessings (small and big) that He sends your way.

Anything less is ungratefulness and shrinks you and your purpose. To enlarge yourself and your purpose, step into gratefulness and an attitude of praise and thanksgiving. By doing so you change the frequency of your mind and state of your heart to be open to and attract good things to you.

When you become a magnet for God's goodness, blessings begin to flow and come your way. Why not? When you praise and glorify God in heaven for that which He has done, is doing and will do with you on earth; it is not surprising that our heavenly Father wants to do good things for you.

God likes to be praised (no less than we who are earthly fathers). Therefore when we express thanks, gratitude and praise to God, we further open God's heart to keep being good to, blessing, and wonderfully surprising us. Keep praising God and encouraging Him to show off!

Even by being grateful in seasons of suffering, we attract and give way to the wisdom of God to teach us how to live large and in charge no matter the challenge. In so doing, God can turn the situation, problem and mess around for us causing us to abound, succeed and excel in all things.

Every mess is potentially a message in the making; every stumbling block a potential stepping stone; every hurt a means to feel and heal others; and problems are just opportunities waiting to be solved.

Many successful people make a good living solving problems. Mechanics solve car problems. Doctors attempt to solve health problems. Fitness trainers solve obesity problems. Dentists solve teeth problems. Babysitters solve parental burnout problems so mom and dad can go on a date, or have some "me time" free from cartoons or teenage drama.

As one of my good friends says, "Thank God for stupid people, because if everyone were smart, we would have to work harder." Dumb people who sometimes drive us nuts are also a blessing in that they enable us to solve the very problems they cause.

Therefore instead of being a murmurer and complainer, be a problem solver. Many are they who create and complain about problems, but to have integrity of heart you must be forward thinking and a problem solver.

Don't be part of the problem. Be the one who helps engineer solutions. Be forward thinking, innovative and entrepreneurial. As you do, God the Creator of the universe will give you creative ideas to solve problems, help people, lighten their load, and be a blessing.

Of course as you commit to being a blessing and solving problems, God in turn will likewise bless you. It's only natural and expected that the more you serve and show yourself to be a blessing, the more in turn you yourself will be blessed.

Therefore no matter where you find yourself, regardless of the situation and people; be thankful and look for what God is trying to say and do in and through you.

'In everything give thanks: for this is the will of God' concerning you (1Thessalonians 5:18).

Thus YOU are GOD'S WILL. So if circumstances test you, know God is with you and ready to bless you! But rather than being reactive to the circumstances, situation, problem or people; be proactive and lead with vision to be a problem solver.

Be thankful for the problems that appear in your life, because they will teach and enlighten you; causing you to be wiser and sharpen your skill set. A murmuring mindset however will short-circuit your ability to focus, solve problems, and be a blessing.

Murmurers and complainers have an entitlement mentality, but nowhere did God say or promise to us that life would be easy. Life has and comes with many challenges, but if we approach these challenges joyfully and allow them to better us; we will always come out on top and have a testimony from every test we pass through.

Turn your present test into a learning opportunity and future testimony to give God glory. Be thankful, grateful and keep stepping into greatness to allow God to daily show off in and through you!

12. EXCELLENCE

Be a lifelong learner, always growing, and endeavoring to be better. Daily strive to be your best and cultivate excellence. By doing so your integrity will continually be strengthened and you will grow as a person.

Nobody likes to be around a halfhearted person without passion. People lacking passion rarely get asked out on dates or to social events.

People who are emotionally flat, lack vision, and live halfhearted rarely do much to change or improve our world.

On the other hand people with passion can move heaven and earth to give birth to newness of life. Despite the lack of education, connections (relational or professional) and finances: passionate people are enjoyable to be around and inspire us.

I've seen janitors cleaning gym bathrooms with jovial dispositions and joyful countenances I genuinely enjoyed talking to. Peace and joy are contagious!

When you can be content and grateful no matter where you find yourself, as you step into greatness, a spirit of excellence will permeate and saturate all you say and do.

Such a spirit of excellence causes you to take pride in all you do, the way you dress, carry yourself, walk and talk. I'm not saying you have to dress a certain way. You be your best and do it with elegance, grace and class.

I personally don't enjoy wearing ties, but do when I have to for speaking engagements and business meetings. Whatever you do, happily do so. Work with a spirit of excellence because somewhere someone is watching (certainly God in heaven who has the hearts of all in His mighty hands) and potentially could promote and entrust you with more if you show yourself faithful in little (even when nobody is watching).

Jesus said, when we are faithful with little, God can entrust us with more and greater things. 'He that is faithful in that which is least is faithful also in much: and he that is unjust in the least is unjust also in much' (Luke 16:10).

Therefore if you are unfaithful in the small, seemingly insignificant tasks like taking out the trash in your home; how can God entrust you with a worldwide ministry, multinational company, life-changing invention, patentable technology, or a scholarship to pursue a PhD?

The principle here is the importance of being excellent in all we say and do. This includes our attitude too. Because if we are obedient outwardly, but inwardly hostile and angrily doing something merely out of obligation, it will eventually be seen and felt in our mannerisms and conduct.

God therefore says if we are willing and obedient, we will eat the good of the land wherever we find ourselves and enter His blessing (see Isaiah 1:19). Too often we are obedient, but inwardly grumbling, defiant and belittling our parents, employers, or the authorities over us.

It's like when I was a teenager and my stepmother asked me to do the dishes. I would obey and do what I was told, but inwardly I was angry and murmuring sometimes. Although I didn't know it at the time, my stepmother could most likely see my displeasure on my face and nonverbally read my feelings.

Of course she never let up (for which I'm today thankful, because I'm a disciplined and hardworking person). Yet at the time when I was learning discipline and having to do things I didn't particularly care for; it was tough and sometimes brutal as I struggled to harness myself within and hold my tongue from lashing out against her.

A spirit of excellence looks for the good and opportunities for personal growth and creativity in all things. Surely many comedians have done scenes on their shows from time spent in the kitchen cooking and cleaning.

Sometimes in the quietness of working is when I get ideas for poems, books, motivational talks, inventions, or places where I'd like to travel. So even times of work can be fun and enriching if we will release the tension within and work happily with a spirit of excellence.

Remember what you resist will often persist. So holding toxic emotions within and resisting work, which we all must do, doesn't serve you well.

Alternatively embracing the tasks and daily chores we all must do with joy and a spirit of excellence lightens the emotional load within and enables you to get them done more easily and quickly.

Don't fight against yourself by being angry and burning yourself up within. Be congruent body-mind-spirit and when you agree to do something, do it wholeheartedly with a spirit of excellence.

A double-minded person is unstable in all of their ways (James 1:8). Don't allow instability of thought, character or conduct to find any place in you. Cultivate a spirit of excellence and live happily; large and in charge in all you touch and do!

As you cultivate and live with a spirit of excellence; creative ideas, promotions and countless blessings await you!

I truly and wholeheartedly believe when we get our hearts right and live with integrity, God will bless us in innumerable ways and set miracles in motion on our behalf and bless us.

Paul F. Davis is a worldwide motivational speaker, global business consultant, corporate trainer, life coach, spiritual teacher and author who has touched 70 countries building bridges cross-culturally empowering people throughout the earth to transcend their limitations and live their dreams!

Paul speaks for corporations, universities, churches, the military and several luxury cruise lines at sea. Paul has appeared on numerous international broadcasts from *Investors Business Daily*, *Oprah and Friends* to *Fox News* to talk about success, leadership, relational intricacies, conflict resolution, life balance and overcoming adversity.

Playboy Radio Afternoon Advice host Tiffany Granath calls Paul an "awesome" relational coach and recommends his books on love, dating, and sexuality.

Paul worked at Ground Zero in NYC during the first week of 9/11; helped rebuild a home at the tsunami epicenter in Indonesia; comforted victims of genocide in Rwanda; spoke to leaders in East Timor during the war before UN recognition and independence; inspired students and monks in Myanmar; promoted peace, religious tolerance and reconciliation in Pakistan (after 9/11 and before Presidents Bush and Obama pursued Bin Laden therein); developed leaders deep in the bush of rural war-torn east Africa; and fed the hungry in impoverished Haiti.

Paul studied global affairs in grad school at NYU, conflict resolution and mediation at Hofstra Law School, negotiations at Harvard Business School & the University of Washington School of Business, global food law at Michigan State College of Law, personal fitness with the Aerobics Fitness Association of America, NLP & Life Coaching, advanced interrogation, peacemaking, debt arbitration, and studied as an undergrad at UCF.

Paul enjoys yoga, weight lifting, nutrition, surfing, swimming, snorkeling, tennis, baseball, college football, spas, massage, cruise ships, island hopping and exploring new countries.

Paul's heartfelt and humorous stories from around the world empower people to love passionately and fearlessly live their dreams.

http://www.PaulFDavis.com

info @ PaulFDavis.com – contact Paul for life coaching, business consulting or to schedule Paul to speak in your city!

Paul ministering in Brasilia, the capital of Brazil.

Paul speaking in Ecuador.

www.ingramcontent.com/pod-product-compliance
Lightning Source LLC
Chambersburg PA
CBHW021411170526
45164CB00002B/605